Mary Wilder Tileston

Great Souls at Prayer

Fourteen Centuries of Prayer, Praise and Aspiration, from St. Augustine...

Mary Wilder Tileston

Great Souls at Prayer
Fourteen Centuries of Prayer, Praise and Aspiration, from St. Augustine...

ISBN/EAN: 9783337180911

Printed in Europe, USA, Canada, Australia, Japan

Cover: Foto ©Thomas Meinert / pixelio.de

More available books at **www.hansebooks.com**

GREAT SOULS AT PRAYER

GREAT SOULS AT PRAYER

FOURTEEN CENTURIES OF PRAYER, PRAISE AND ASPIRATION, FROM ST. AUGUSTINE TO CHRISTINA ROSSETTI AND ROBERT LOUIS STEVENSON

Selected and Arranged
By Mrs. MARY W. TILESTON
AUTHOR OF "DAILY STRENGTH FOR DAILY NEEDS"

LONDON: JAMES BOWDEN
10 HENRIETTA STREET W.C
1898

Preface

This collection of prayers for daily use has been gathered from many sources, ancient and modern. It has historical interest, and the literary quality has been carefully considered, but the primary object is to nourish the spiritual life. As the design is to provide a brief selection for every day, in many cases a portion only of a long prayer is given, or it is condensed by omission, but alterations have been made as sparingly as possible.

Fourteen centuries of prayer, aspiration, and praise unite here in one harmony of devotion. A large number of these prayers date from the fifth and sixth centuries, taken from the Leonine, Gelasian, and Gregorian Sacramentaries, from which the collects in the Book of Common Prayer are in great measure derived.

Preface

The earnest and impassioned prayers of St. Augustine belong to the same period. Many of the prayers attributed to him, however, are of later origin and doubtful authorship, some of them, probably, being by St. Anselm and St. Bernard. There are some striking and fervent collects from the Mozarabic Sacramentary, which was in use in Spain before A. D. 700. In the Middle Ages, St. Anselm, Thomas à Kempis, and others contribute devout prayers, and the age of the Reformation in England and Germany is very rich in devotional treasures. In the succeeding centuries, Bishop Andrewes, Jeremy Taylor, Bishop Wilson, Dr. Johnson, and many others, continue the golden chain down to the present century. The names of Christina G. Rossetti, George Dawson, Rowland Williams, and E. B. Pusey are enough to show that the spirit of prayer still burns with a steady flame.

I acknowledge, with gratitude, my indebtedness to "Ancient Collects," by Rev. William Bright; Bunsen's "Collec-

Preface

tion of Prayers"; "Annus Domini," and "The Face of the Deep," by Miss Rossetti; "Prayers," by George Dawson; "Private Prayers," by Rev. E. B. Pusey; "Psalms and Litanies," by Rev. Rowland Williams; "Home Prayers," by Rev. James Martineau; "Moments on the Mount," and "Voices of the Spirit," by Rev. George Matheson; "Prayers," by Rev. Rufus Ellis, and others too numerous to mention. I am indebted to Rev. J. R. Miller for a prayer contributed by him to this book. I must also express my thanks to the publishers who have kindly given me permission to use copyrighted material; to Messrs. Armstrong & Son, for prayers from the works of Dr. Matheson, above mentioned; and to Mr. Charles Baxter for the prayers by Robert Louis Stevenson.

Mary Wilder Tileston.

The Publisher desires to express his thanks to the Society for the Promotion of Christian Knowledge for permission to use several prayers from "The Face of the Deep," by the late Christina Rossetti, and to Messrs. James Parker & Sons for the use of the extracts from "Annus Domini," by the same Author.

Index of Subjects

Adversity or Danger—78, 84, 109, 118, 151, 230, 278, 284, 288, 341, 351, 358.

Affliction and Suffering—30, 31, 79, 96, 98, 145, 146, 158, 167, 170, 223, 245, 250, 258, 263, 264, 269, 273, 308, 315, 316, 327, 331, 338, 345, 350, 352, 364.

Aspiration—4, 8, 40, 64, 65, 100, 103, 108, 110, 116, 122, 125, 127, 134, 144, 147, 148, 154, 162, 168, 179, 181, 189, 197, 199, 220, 240, 261, 265, 266, 270, 281, 290, 296, 302, 308, 320, 328, 329, 346, 360.

Conformity to the Will of God—3, 15, 21, 23, 29, 34, 49, 66, 74, 84, 92, 101, 131, 135, 172, 184, 190, 200, 257, 288, 301, 305, 322, 329, 339, 342.

Courage, Cheerfulness, Strength—1, 10, 18, 33, 88, 95, 102, 133, 142, 145, 151, 176, 177, 179, 191, 205, 230, 237, 246, 247, 275, 280, 285, 311, 319, 323, 324, 349, 354.

Index of Subjects

Confession and Penitence—13, 23, 32, 57, 61, 63, 67, 69, 75, 77, 81, 83, 87, 106, 112, 113, 115, 117, 130, 133, 137, 140, 157, 160, 175, 188, 208, 224, 254, 268, 300, 304, 330.

Consecration and Holiness—19, 33, 40, 42, 60, 82, 86, 109, 122, 165, 201, 206, 226, 238, 242, 244, 266, 272, 275, 300, 310, 322, 330, 336, 337, 340, 347, 353, 361.

Communion of Saints—3, 25, 59, 100, 139, 150, 168, 186, 192, 306, 307, 359.

Duty—1, 7, 22, 24, 31, 34, 39, 45, 46, 58, 86, 91, 93, 95, 99, 139, 142, 146, 173, 177, 185, 194, 213, 214, 249, 253, 274, 282, 283, 287, 289, 300, 303, 309, 314, 322, 328, 339.

Faith and Fervor—8, 16, 25, 35, 51, 62, 70, 105, 111, 178.

Forgiveness and Kindness—26, 38, 55, 87, 119, 121, 125, 130, 136, 159, 162, 171, 193, 195, 204, 207, 212, 225, 227, 232, 251, 286, 362.

Guidance and Light—6, 15, 22, 28, 40, 44, 62, 80, 81, 129, 138, 149, 180, 183, 190, 194, 196, 213, 215, 237, 246, 248, 253, 312, 313, 344.

Love of Family, Friends, Mankind—5, 24, 48, 54, 58, 66, 67, 76, 97, 104, 107, 115, 119, 120, 121, 127, 169, 183, 193, 203, 216, 226, 232, 239, 249, 263, 269, 285, 286, 296, 297, 309, 315, 321, 335, 356, 357, 357.

Index of Subjects

Love of God—16, 17, 37, 52, 54, 66, 67, 73, 90, 95, 97, 104, 105, 108, 120, 141, 153, 176, 178, 182, 192, 195, 218, 222, 232, 234, 235, 267, 287, 297, 298, 305, 313, 315, 317, 332, 363.

Obedience to God—5, 7, 16, 20, 26, 55, 60, 91, 97, 109, 123, 135, 140, 143, 178, 182, 202, 221, 233, 243, 248, 325, 329.

Peace and Rest in God—8, 10, 14, 18, 21, 25, 43, 52, 54, 59, 72, 96, 104, 126, 136, 143, 171, 195, 203, 223, 240, 255, 260, 284, 314, 318, 362.

Purity and Truth—26, 47, 85, 99, 103, 111, 123, 147, 155, 164, 207, 234, 243, 262, 289, 330.

Submission and Resignation—36, 41, 58, 71, 89, 96, 102, 132, 164, 170, 210, 219, 236, 241, 252, 276, 292, 304, 334, 338, 363.

Temptation and Trial—90, 133, 137, 166, 235, 265, 298.

Thanksgiving and Praise—9, 11, 12, 27, 48, 50, 56, 68, 94, 124, 141, 150, 152, 156, 163, 174, 211, 228, 231, 238, 256, 280, 281, 294, 295, 301, 323, 326, 306.

Trust in God—2, 28, 41, 46, 53, 92, 94, 114, 128, 161, 186, 187, 198, 202, 209, 218, 219, 228, 229, 236, 247, 252, 259, 270, 271, 277, 293, 299, 321, 333, 341, 343, 348, 355, 356, 358, 365.

Index of Authors

Aitken, Rev. William Hay Hunter, b. 1841—336

Albrecht, Rev. Bernhard (1569-1636)—162

Alcuinus, Albinus Flaccus (735-804)—13

Alford, Rev. Henry (1810-1871)—26, 54, 60, 90, 135, 159, 185.

Altar at Home, The 1862—277.

Ambrose, St. (340-397)—287.

Ancient Collect—351.

Andrewes, Bishop Lancelot (1555-1626)—112, 156, 198, 220, 264, 290.

Anselm, St. (1033-1109)—17, 120, 354.

Aquinas, St. Thomas (1225?-1274)—42.

Arndt, Rev. Johann (1555-1621)—37, 87, 134, 212.

Arnold, Rev. Gottfried (1665-1714)—154.

Arnold, Rev. Thomas (1795-1842)—7, 86, 127.

Augustine, St. (354-430)—2, 52, 57, 61, 75, 108, 116, 138, 160, 182, 196, 222, 256, 278, 312, 336, 344.

Index of Authors

Basil, St. (329-379)—55.

Becon, Rev. Thomas (1511-1570)—24, 50.

Bersier, Rev. Eugène (1831-1889)—133, 263, 285, 331.

Besson, Rev. Charles Jean Baptiste (1816-1861)—241.

Book of Christian Prayers, A 1578—66, 126.

Book of Common Prayer, 1549—321.

Book of Common Prayer, 1626—296.

Book of Hours, 1865—144, 178, 183, 285.

Book of Prayers, 1851—262, 359.

Bright, Rev. William, b. 1824—15, 46, 62, 107.

Bunsen's Collection—48, 67.

Carpenter, Mary, (1807-1877)—43.

Channing, Rev. William Ellery (1780-1842)—323.

Collyer, Rev. Robert, b. 1823—187, 228, 229.

Coptic Liturgy of St. Cyril—119, 147.

Dawson, Rev. George (1821-1876)—1, 8, 28, 41, 51, 59, 84, 91, 97, 117, 123, 129, 143, 149, 155, 161, 167, 189, 205, 213, 223, 233, 247, 259, 271, 283, 293, 299, 319, 333, 341.

Doddridge, Rev. Philip (1702-1751)—238.

Donne, Rev. John (1573-1631)—250.

Index of Authors

Ellis, Rev. Rufus (1819-1885)—56, 150, 203, 307.

Embden, Rev. Joachim (1595-1650)—59.

Erasmus, Desiderius (1467-1536)—180.

Fénelon, Archbishop François de la Mothe (1651-1715)—29, 132.

Foote, Rev. Henry Wilder (1838-1889)—65, 273, 295, 325, 345, 358.

Gallican Sacramentary, A.D. 800—60, 263.

Gelasian Sacramentary, A.D. 492 or 494—10, 85, 91, 114, 140, 161, 203, 262, 284, 287, 300, 304, 323, 331, 341, 350, 355, 357.

Gothic Missal—25.

Goulburn's Family Prayers—137.

Greek Church—68, 106, 124, 240.

Gregorian Sacramentary, A.D. 590—6, 84, 99, 217, 289, 312, 314.

Grey, Lady Jane (1537-1554)—118.

Habermann, Johann (1516-1590)—352.

Hare, Mrs. Maria (1798-1870)—20, 67, 173, 201, 261.

Henry, Rev. Matthew (1662-1714)—282.

Henry VIII's Primer, 1545—27, 94.

Hickes' Devotions, 1700—216, 284, 322.

Index of Authors

How, Charles (1661-1745)—82, 135, 153, 298, 329, 366.

Hunter's Devotional Services, 1892—270, 297.

Jacobite Liturgy of St. Dionysius—104.

Jenks, Rev. Benjamin (1646-1714)—121, 179, 288, 314, 324, 337, 357.

Jerome, St. (345?-420)—224.

Johnson, Samuel (1709-1784)—22, 77, 146, 208, 248, 302.

Kempis, Thomas à (1379-1471)—14, 21, 34, 41, 64, 73, 92, 130, 158, 166, 188, 210, 230, 254, 268, 280, 292, 304, 308, 320, 330, 338, 350, 356.

Kepler, Johann (1571-1630)—231.

King's Chapel Liturgy, 1831—137, 237.

Leighton, Archbishop Robert (1611-1684)—353.

Leonine Sacramentary, A.D. 440—31, 109, 165, 191, 243, 280, 315, 362.

Liturgy of St. James (2d century?)—19.

Liturgy of St. Mark (175-254)—81, 98, 152, 223.

Martineau, Rev. James, b. 1805—12, 30, 69, 83, 93, 115, 139, 181, 180, 200, 240, 275, 303, 356.

Index of Authors

Martineau's Common Prayer for Christian Worship—45.

Martyn, Rev. Henry (1781-1812)—31.

Matheson, Rev. George, b. 1842—3, 72, 101, 131, 197, 215, 257, 349.

Mayer, Rev. Christ.—242.

Melancthon, Rev. Philip (1497-1560)—168.

Miller, Rev. James Russell, b. 1840—311.

Monsell, Rev. John Samuel Bewley (1811-1875)—25.

Mozarabic Sacramentary, before A.D. 700—1, 22, 24, 62, 80, 102, 136, 171, 190, 269, 328, 354, 363.

Nelson, Robert (1656-1715)—102.

New Church Book of Worship, 1876—194, 225, 252.

Newman, Cardinal John (1801-1890)—35, 80, 109, 165, 211, 219, 255, 334, 343.

Osgood, Rev. Samuel (1812-1880)—360.

Oxenden, Bishop Ashton (1808-1892)—163, 227, 251, 279, 313.

Palma, Ludovicus—244.

Paradise for the Christian Soul—111, 176, 200, 338.

Index of Authors

Pascal, Blaise (1623-1662)—89.

Patrick, Bishop Simon (1626-1707)—11, 206, 342, 361.

Penitent Pilgrim, The, 1641—362.

Pocket Manual of Prayers, 1860—234, 328.

Priest's Prayer Book—1870, 123, 337.

Private Devotions, 1560—32, 234, 266, 306, 344.

Pusey, Rev. Edward Bouverie (1800-1882)—10, 18, 36, 49, 74, 88, 97, 105, 108, 141, 147, 155, 170, 175, 183, 190, 217, 235, 239, 267, 270, 281, 296, 301, 313, 317, 332.

Quirsfeld, Rev. Johann (1641-1686)—339.

Reinhard, Rev. V. R. (1753-1812)—110.

Ridley, Bishop Nicholas (1500?-1555)—151, 246.

Ritter, Melchior, 1689—260.

Roman Breviary—2, 7, 8, 18, 23, 32, 46, 88, 90, 96, 115, 122, 142, 145, 177, 185, 194, 202, 218, 247, 253, 266, 288, 297, 346.

Rossetti, Christina Georgina (1830-1895)—5, 16, 23, 28, 34, 36, 40, 48, 55, 58, 63, 66, 70, 81, 89, 92, 94, 99, 111, 119, 125, 128, 133, 142, 146, 151, 159, 164, 168, 169, 171, 177, 182, 184, 191, 195, 207, 218, 225, 231, 237, 240, 246, 253,

Index of Authors

Rossetti, Christina Georgina (1830-1895)—Continued
269, 281, 289, 305, 309, 315, 321, 329, 340, 345, 351, 355, 363.

Sailer, Rev. Michael (1751-1832)—174, 272.

Sarum Breviary, 1085—6, 26, 44, 54, 63, 71, 95, 106, 132, 143, 153, 176, 207, 213, 218, 224, 230, 232, 268, 275, 280, 300, 308, 320, 330, 347.

Scheretz, Rev. S. (1584-1639)—364.

Shaftesbury, **Antony** Ashley Cooper, **Earl of** (1801-1885)—335.

Sidney, Sir Philip (1554-1586)—30.

Skinner, Rev. James (1818-1882)—125, 309, 339.

Stark, J. F. (1680-1756)—76, 316.

Stevenson, Robert Louis (1850-1894)—4, 95.

Stone, Rev. **Thomas Treadwell** (1801-1895)—193.

Syrian Clementine Liturgy—195.

Taylor, Bishop Jeremy (1613-1667)—9, 16, 38, 58, 70, 85, 107, 114, 128, 140, 178, 202, 214, 274, 294, 310, 326, 340, 348.

Tersteegen, Gerhard (1697-1769)—33, 100, 148, 192, 226.

Theresa, St. (1515-1583)—15.

Index of Authors

Treasury of Devotion, 1869—44, 103, 122, 144, 204, 232, 235, 252, 258, 301, 347.

Vives, Ludovicus, 1578—239, 249, 286.

Way of Eternal Life, The—172, 318.

Weiss, Rev. S. (1738-1805)—236, 276.

Williams, Rev. Rowland (1818-1870)—5, 40, 47, 70, 78, 103, 113, 145, 157, 170, 199, 221, 243, 248, 265, 291, 300, 305, 327, 346.

Wilson, Bishop Thomas (1663-1755)—53, 71, 96, 104, 136, 140, 164, 170, 184, 267, 322, 326.

Woolman, John (1720-1772)—245.

Zschokke, Johann Heinrich (1771-1848)—365.

January the First ✛ ✛ ✛ ✛ ✛ ✛ ✛ ✛ 1

Almighty God, have mercy upon us, who, when troubled with the things that are past, lose faith, and life, and courage, and hope. So have mercy upon us, and uphold us, that we, being sustained by a true faith that Thou art merciful and forgiving, may go on in the life of the future to keep Thy commandments, to rejoice in Thy bounty, to trust in Thy mercy, and to hope in the eternal life. Grant unto all of us, whatsoever may betide us, to remember ever that it is all of Thy guidance, under Thy care, by Thy will; that so, in darkest days, beholding Thee we may have courage to go on, faith to endure, patience to bear, and hopefulness to hold out, even unto the end—Amen.
George Dawson.

✠

O Thou, who art ever the same, grant us so to pass through the coming year with faithful hearts, that we may be able in all things to please Thy loving eyes—Amen.
Mozarabic, 700 A. D.

January the Second

Lord our God, under the shadow of Thy wings let us hope. Thou wilt support us, both when little, and even to gray hairs. When our strength is of Thee, it is strength; but, when our own, it is feebleness. We return unto Thee, O Lord, that from their weariness our souls may rise towards Thee, leaning on the things which Thou hast created, and passing on to Thyself, who hast wonderfully made them; for with Thee is refreshment and true strength—Amen.

St. Augustine.

God, let the sighing of the prisoner come before Thee, and mercifully grant unto us that we may be delivered by Thine almighty power from all bonds and chains of sin whether in our bodies or in our souls, through Jesus Christ our Lord—Amen.

Roman Breviary.

January the Third — 3

My Father, help me as a follower of Christ to say, "Thy will be done." Thou wouldest not have me accept Thy will because I *must*, but because I *may*. Thou wouldest have me take it, not with resignation, but with joy, not with the absence of murmur, but with the song of praise. How shall I reach this goal? I shall only reach it by feeling what the Psalmist felt—that Thy will comes from a "good Spirit," and goes towards a "land of uprightness." Teach me that Thy will is love; teach me that Thy love is wise. Guide me not blindfold, but with open eyes. Grant me the power to look both behind and before—behind to "Thy good Spirit," before to "the land of uprightness." Give me the blessedness of the man whose delight is in Thy law, who can tell of Thy statutes rejoicing the heart. I shall obey Thy will in perfect freedom when I can say, "Thy Spirit is good"—Amen.

George Matheson.

January the Fourth

We beseech Thee, Lord, to behold us with favor, folk of many families and nations gathered together in the peace of this roof, weak men and women subsisting under the covert of Thy patience. Be patient still; suffer us yet a while longer—with our broken purposes of good, with our idle endeavors against evil, suffer us a while longer to endure and (if it may be) help us to do better. Bless to us our extraordinary mercies; if the day come when these must be taken, brace us to play the man under affliction. Be with our friends, be with ourselves. Go with each of us to rest; if any awake, temper to them the dark hours of watching; and when the day returns, return to us, our sun and comforter, and call us up with morning faces and with morning hearts—eager to labor—eager to be happy, if happiness shall be our portion—and if the day be marked for sorrow, strong to endure it—Amen.

Robert Louis Stevenson.

January the Fifth ✢ ✢ ✢ ✢ ✢ ✢ ✢ ✢ 5

O God, the Enlightener of men, who of all graces givest the most abundant blessing upon heavenly love ; we beseech Thee to cleanse us from selfishness, and grant us, for Thy love, so to love our brethren that we may be Thy children upon earth ; and thereby, walking in Thy truth, attain to Thy unspeakable joy, who art the Giver of life to all who truly love Thee. Grant this prayer, O Lord— Amen.

Rowland Williams.

Make us of quick and tender conscience, O Lord ; that understanding we may obey every word of Thine, and discerning may follow every suggestion of Thine indwelling Spirit. Speak, Lord, for Thy servant heareth—Amen.

Christina G. Rossetti.

6 ✠ ✠ ✠ ✠ ✠ ✠ ✠ ✠ January the Sixth

We beseech Thee, O Lord, let our hearts be graciously enlightened by Thy holy radiance, that we may serve Thee without fear in holiness and righteousness all the days of our life; that so we may escape the darkness of this world, and by Thy guidance attain the land of eternal brightness; through Thy mercy, O blessed Lord, Who dost live and govern all things, world without end—Amen.

Sarum Breviary, A. D. 1085.

Almighty and everlasting God, the Brightness of faithful souls, fill the world with Thy glory, we pray Thee, and show Thyself, by the radiance of Thy light, to all the nations of the world, through Jesus Christ, our Lord—Amen.

Gregorian Sacramentary, A. D. 590.

January the Seventh + + + + + + + 7

lmighty and everlasting God, grant that our wills be ever meekly subject to Thy will, and our hearts be ever honestly ready to serve Thee—Amen.

Roman Breviary.

 Lord, grant that my heart may be truly cleansed and filled with Thy Holy Spirit, and that I may arise to serve Thee, and lie down to sleep in entire confidence in Thee, and submission to Thy will, ready for life or for death. Let me live for the day, not overcharged with worldly cares, but feeling that my treasure is not here, and desiring truly to be joined to Thee in Thy heavenly kingdom, and to those who are already gone to Thee. O Lord, save me from sin, and guide me with Thy Spirit, and keep me in faithful obedience to Thee, through Jesus Christ Thy Son, our Lord—Amen.

Thomas Arnold.

8 ✢ ✢ ✢ ✢ ✢ ✢ ✢ January the Eighth

Grant unto us, Almighty God, of Thy good Spirit, that quiet heart, and that patient lowliness to which Thy comforting Spirit comes; that we, being humble toward Thee, and loving toward one another, may have our hearts prepared for that peace of Thine which passeth understanding; which, if we have, the storms of life can hurt us but little, and the cares of life vex us not at all; in presence of which death shall lose its sting, and the grave its terror; and we, in calm joy, walk all the days of our appointed time, until our great change shall come—Amen.

George Dawson.

God, mercifully grant unto us that the fire of Thy love may burn up in us all things that displease Thee, and make us meet for Thy heavenly kingdom—Amen.

Roman Breviary.

January the Ninth ✢ ✢ ✢ ✢ ✢ ✢ ✢ ✢ 9

Most merciful and gracious God, Thou Fountain of all mercy and blessing, Thou hast opened the hand of Thy mercy to fill me with blessings, and the sweet effects of Thy loving-kindness. Thou feedest us like a Shepherd, Thou lovest us as a Friend, and thinkest on us perpetually, as a careful mother on her helpless babe, and art exceeding merciful to all that fear Thee. As Thou hast spread Thy hand upon me for a covering, so also enlarge my heart with thankfulness; and let Thy gracious favors and loving-kindness endure for ever and ever upon Thy servant; and grant that what Thou hast sown in mercy, may spring up in duty; and let Thy grace so strengthen my purposes that I may sin no more, but walk in the paths of Thy commandments; that I, living here to the glory of Thy name, may at last enter into the glory of my Lord, to spend a whole eternity in giving praise to Thy ever-glorious name—Amen.

Jeremy Taylor.

January the Tenth

Let me not seek out of Thee what I can find only in Thee, O Lord, peace and rest and joy and bliss, which abide only in Thine abiding joy. Lift up my soul above the weary round of harassing thoughts to Thy eternal Presence. Lift up my soul to the pure, bright, serene, radiant atmosphere of Thy Presence, that there I may breathe freely, there repose in Thy love, there be at rest from myself, and from all things that weary me; and thence return, arrayed with Thy peace, to do and bear what shall please Thee— Amen.

E. B. Pusey.

O God, forasmuch as our strength is in Thee, mercifully grant that Thy Holy Spirit may in all things direct and rule our hearts, through Jesus Christ our Lord— Amen.

Gelasian Sacramentary, A.D. 492.

January the Eleventh ✛ ✛ ✛ ✛ ✛ ✛ 11

Almighty and most merciful Father, in whom we live and move and have our being, to whose tender compassion we owe our safety in days past, together with all the comforts of this present life, and the hopes of that which is to come ; we praise Thee, O God, our Creator ; unto Thee do we give thanks, O God our exceeding Joy, who daily pourest Thy benefits upon us. Grant, we beseech Thee, that Jesus our Lord, the Hope of glory, may be formed in us, in all humility, meekness, patience, contentedness, and absolute surrender of our souls and bodies to Thy holy will and pleasure. Leave us not, nor forsake us, O Father, but conduct us safe through all changes of our condition here, in an unchangeable love to Thee, and in holy tranquillity of mind in Thy love to us, till we come to dwell with Thee, and rejoice in Thee forever—Amen.

Simon Patrick (1626-1707).

January the Twelfth

**Source of Life and Strength!** many of Thy mercies do we plainly see, and we believe in a boundless store behind. No morning stars that sing together can have deeper call than we for grateful joy. Thou hast given us a life of high vocation, and Thine own breathing in our hearts interprets for us its sacred opportunities. Thou hast cheered the way with many dear affections and glimpses of solemn beauty and everlasting truth. Not a cloud of sorrow, but Thou hast touched with glory : not a dusty atmosphere of care, but Thy light shines through! And, lest our spirits should fail before Thine unattainable perfections, Thou hast set us in the train of Thy saints who have learned to take up the cross of sacrifice. Let the time past suffice to have wrought our own will, and now make us consecrate to Thine—Amen.

James Martineau.

January the Thirteenth ✧ ✧ ✧ ✧ ✧ 13

Almighty and merciful God, the Fountain of all goodness, who knowest the thoughts of our hearts, we confess unto Thee that we have sinned against Thee, and done evil in Thy sight. Wash us, we beseech Thee, from the stains of our past sins, and give us grace and power to put away all hurtful things; so that, being delivered from the bondage of sin, we may bring forth worthy fruits of repentance.

O eternal Light, shine into our hearts. O eternal Goodness, deliver us from evil. O eternal Power, be Thou our support. Eternal Wisdom, scatter the darkness of our ignorance. Eternal Pity, have mercy upon us. Grant unto us that with all our hearts, and minds, and strength, we may evermore seek Thy face; and finally bring us, in Thine infinite mercy, to Thy holy presence. So strengthen our weakness that, following in the footsteps of Thy blessed Son, we may obtain Thy mercy, and enter into Thy promised joy —Amen.

Alcuin, A. D. 780.

Grant me, O most loving Lord, to rest in Thee above all creatures, above all health and beauty, above all glory and honor, above all power and dignity, above all knowledge and subtilty, above all riches and art, above all fame and praise, above all sweetness and comfort, above all hope and promise, above all gifts and favors that Thou canst give and impart to us, above all jubilee that the mind of man can receive and feel; finally, above angels and archangels, and above all the heavenly host, above all things visible and invisible, and above all that Thou art not, O my God. It is too small and unsatisfying, whatsoever Thou bestowest on me apart from Thee, or revealest to me, or promisest, whilst Thou art not seen, and not fully obtained. For surely my heart cannot truly rest, nor be entirely contented, unless it rest in Thee —Amen.

Thomas à Kempis.

January the Fifteenth ✢ ✢ ✢ ✢ ✢ ✢ 15

O God, by whom the meek are guided in judgment, and light riseth up in darkness for the godly; grant us, in all our doubts and uncertainties, the grace to ask what Thou wouldest have us to do; that the Spirit of wisdom may save us from all false choices, and that in Thy light we may see light, and in Thy straight path may not stumble, through Jesus Christ our Lord—Amen.

William Bright.

Govern all by Thy wisdom, O Lord, so that my soul may always be serving Thee as Thou dost will, and not as I may choose. Do not punish me, I beseech Thee, by granting that which I wish or ask, if it offend Thy love, which would always live in me. Let me die to myself, that so I may serve Thee: let me live to Thee, who in Thyself art the true Life—Amen.

St. Theresa (1515-1583).

16 ✢ ✢ ✢ ✢ ✢ January the Sixteenth

O Lord, my God, Fountain of all true and holy love; who hast made me, and preserved me, that I might love Thee; give to Thy servant such a love, that whatsoever in Thy service may happen contrary to flesh and blood, I may not feel it; that humility may be my sanctuary, and Thy service the joy of my soul, and death itself the entrance of an eternal life, when I may live with Thee, my Strength and my Refuge, my God and everlasting Hope—Amen.

Jeremy Taylor.

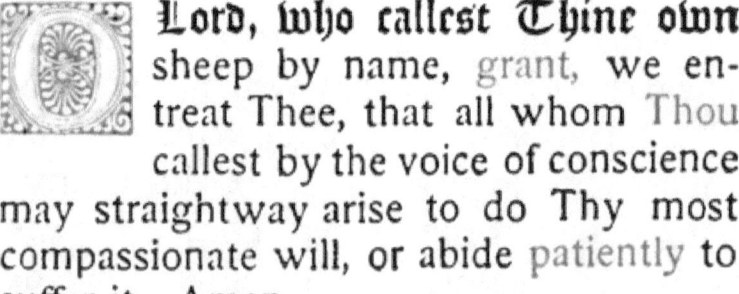O Lord, who callest Thine own sheep by name, grant, we entreat Thee, that all whom Thou callest by the voice of conscience may straightway arise to do Thy most compassionate will, or abide patiently to suffer it—Amen.

Christina G. Rossetti.

January the Seventeenth ✦ ✦ ✦ ✦ 17

 **God, Thou art Life, Wisdom,** Truth, Bounty, and Blessedness, the Eternal, the only true Good! My God and my Lord, Thou art my hope and my heart's joy. I confess, with thanksgiving, that Thou hast made me in Thine image, that I may direct all my thoughts to Thee, and love Thee. Lord, make me to know Thee aright, that I may more and more love, and enjoy, and possess Thee. And since, in the life here below, I cannot fully attain this blessedness, let it at least grow in me day by day, until it all be fulfilled at last in the life to come. Here be the knowledge of Thee increased, and there let it be perfected. Here let my love to Thee grow, and there let it ripen ; that my joy being here great in hope, may there in fruition be made perfect—Amen.

St. Anselm (1033-1109).

18 ✜ ✛ ✛ ✛ ✛ January the Eighteenth

Lord, without Thee I can do nothing; with Thee I can do all. Help me by Thy grace, that I fall not; help me by Thy strength, to resist mightily the very first beginnings of evil, before it takes hold of me; help me to cast myself at once at Thy sacred feet, and lie still there, until the storm be overpast; and, if I lose sight of Thee, bring me back quickly to Thee, and grant me to love Thee better, for Thy tender mercy's sake—Amen.

E. B. Pusey.

Grant unto us, we beseech Thee, O Almighty God, that we, who seek the shelter of Thy protection, being defended from all evils, may serve Thee in peace and quietness of spirit, through Jesus Christ our Lord—Amen.

Roman Breviary.

January the Nineteenth + + + + + 19

O God, the Father of our Saviour Jesus Christ, whose name is great, whose nature is blissful, whose goodness is inexhaustible, God and Ruler of all things, who art blessed forever; before whom stand thousands and thousands, and ten thousand times ten thousand, the hosts of holy angels and archangels; sanctify, O Lord, our souls and bodies and spirits, search our consciences, and cast out of us every evil thought, every base desire, all envy and pride, all wrath and anger, and all that is contrary to Thy holy will. And grant us, O Lord, Lover of men, with a pure heart and contrite soul, to call upon Thee, our holy God and Father who art in heaven—Amen.

Liturgy of St. James,
2nd Century.

January the Twentieth

Lord, this is all my desire—to walk along the path of life that Thou hast appointed me, even as Jesus my Lord would walk along it, in steadfastness of faith, in meekness of spirit, in lowliness of heart, in gentleness of love. And because outward events have so much power in scattering my thoughts and disturbing the inward peace in which alone the voice of Thy spirit is heard, do Thou, gracious Lord, calm and settle my soul by that subduing power which alone can bring all thoughts and desires of the heart into captivity to Thyself. All I have is Thine; do Thou with all as seems best to Thy divine will; for I know not what is best. Let not the cares or duties of this life press on me too heavily; but lighten my burden, that I may follow Thy way in quietness, filled with thankfulness for Thy mercy, and rendering acceptable service unto Thee— Amen.

Maria Hare.

January the Twenty-first + + + + 21

 **Most merciful Lord, grant to me** Thy grace, that it may be with me, and labor with me, and persevere with me even to the end. Grant that I may always desire and will that which is to Thee most acceptable, and most dear. Let Thy will be mine, and my will ever follow Thine, and agree perfectly with it. Grant to me, above all things that can be desired, to rest in Thee, and in Thee to have my heart at peace. Thou art the true peace of the heart, Thou its only rest; out of Thee all things are hard and restless. In this very peace, that is, in Thee, the one Chiefest Eternal Good, I will sleep and rest— Amen.

Thomas à Kempis.

22 ✢ ✢ ✢ January the Twenty-second

O GOD, with Whom is the well of life, and in Whose light we see light; increase in us, we beseech Thee, the brightness of Divine knowledge, whereby we may be able to reach Thy plenteous fountain; impart to our thirsting souls the draught of life, and restore to our darkened minds the light from heaven—Amen.

Mozarabic, before 700 A.D.

ALMIGHTY God, our heavenly Father, without Whose help labor is useless, without Whose light search is vain, invigorate my studies, and direct my inquiries, that I may, by due diligence and right discernment, establish myself and others in Thy holy faith. Take not, O Lord, Thy Holy Spirit from me; let not evil thoughts have dominion in my mind. Let me not linger in ignorance, but enlighten and support me, for the sake of Jesus Christ our Lord—Amen.

Samuel Johnson.

January the Twenty-third ✦ ✦ ✦ ✦ 23

O God, Who art faithful and just to forgive us our sins, mercifully grant unto us that we may be delivered from the bondage of our sins, and may one day rejoice in perfect liberty in our very Fatherland, which is in heaven—Amen.

Roman Breviary.

O Lord, in Whom is our hope, remove far from us, we pray Thee, empty hopes and presumptuous confidence. Make our hearts so right with Thy most holy and loving heart, that hoping in Thee we may do good ; until that day when faith and hope shall be abolished by sight and possession, and love shall be all in all—Amen.

Christina G. Rossetti.

24 ✦ ✦ ✦ January the Twenty-fourth

Grant, O heavenly Father, that we may so faithfully believe in Thee, and so fervently love one another, alway living in Thy fear, and in the obedience of Thy holy law and blessed will, that we, being fruitful in all good works, may lead our life according to Thy good pleasure in this transitory world and, after this frail and short life, obtain the true and immortal life, where thou livest and reignest, world without end—Amen.

Thomas Becon (1511-1567).

Make us, O Lord, to flourish like pure lilies in the courts of Thine house, and to show forth to the faithful the fragrance of good works, and the example of a godly life, through Thy mercy and grace—Amen.

Mozarabic Sacramentary, before 700 A.D.

January the Twenty-fifth ✣ ✣ ✣ ✣ 25

Almighty and everlasting God, Who dost enkindle the flame of Thy love in the hearts of the saints, grant unto us the same faith and power of love; that, as we rejoice in their triumphs, we may profit by their examples, through Jesus Christ our Lord—Amen.

Gothic Missal.

O Thou, with Whom is the Fountain of Life, and without Whom we can do nothing; Whose grace is sufficient for us, and Whose strength is made perfect in weakness; abide in us, that we, keeping Thy commandments, may abide in Thy love; so shall our peace be as a river, and our righteousness as the waves of the sea; through Jesus Christ our Lord—Amen.

John S. B. Monsell.

26 ✣ ✣ ✣ ✣ January the Twenty-sixth

God, perfect us in love, that we may conquer all selfishness and hatred of others; fill our hearts with Thy joy, and shed abroad in them Thy peace which passeth understanding; that so those murmurings and disputings to which we are too prone may be overcome. Make us long-suffering and gentle, and thus subdue our hastiness and angry tempers, and grant that we may bring forth the blessed fruits of the Spirit, to Thy praise and glory, through Jesus Christ our Lord—Amen.

Henry Alford.

Glorious and Almighty God, in Whom all the spirits of the blessed place the confidence of their hope; grant to us that, by Thy help, we may be able ever to serve Thee with a pure mind, through Christ our Lord—Amen.

Sarum Breviary, A. D. 1085.

January the Twenty-seventh + + + 27

O Merciful Lord God, heavenly Father, I render most high laud, praise, and thanks unto Thee, that Thou hast preserved me both this night, and all the times and days of my life hitherto, under Thy protection; and hast suffered me to live until this present hour. And I beseech Thee heartily that Thou wilt vouchsafe to receive me this day, and the residue of my whole life, from henceforth into Thy good keeping; ruling and governing me with Thy Holy Spirit, that all manner of darkness and evil may be utterly chased and driven out of my heart; and that I may walk in the light of Thy truth, to Thy glory and praise, and to the help and furtherance of my neighbor, through Jesus Christ our Lord and Saviour—Amen.

    Henry VIII's Primer, 1545.

28 ✢ ✢ ✢ January the Twenty-eighth

Almighty God, our Light in darkness, our Strength in weakness, our Hope in sinfulness, and our Eternal Home, be unto us merciful, long-suffering, and patient; that we, who be slow of growth, may hope to come at last to Thy likeness; and, being upheld by Thee, may by Thy mercy go from strength to strength, until, through the waste and dreariness, through the joy and duty of this earthly life having safely passed, we through the fulness of Thy mercy may come into the land of the eternal peace—Amen.

George Dawson.

O Lord, Who seest that all hearts are empty except Thou fill them, and all desires balked except they crave after Thee; give us light and grace to seek and find Thee, that we may be Thine and Thou mayest be ours forever—Amen.

Christina G. Rossetti.

January the Twenty-ninth • • • 29

Lord, I know not what I ought to ask of Thee; Thou only knowest what I need; Thou lovest me better than I know how to love myself. O Father! give to Thy child that which he himself knows not how to ask. I dare not ask either for crosses or consolations; I simply present myself before Thee, I open my heart to Thee. Behold my needs which I know not myself; see and do according to Thy tender mercy. Smite, or heal; depress me, or raise me up; I adore all Thy purposes without knowing them; I am silent; I offer myself in sacrifice; I yield myself to Thee; I would have no other desire than to accomplish Thy will. Teach me to pray. Pray Thyself in me —Amen.

Francois de la Mothe Fénelon.

All-seeing Light, and Eternal Life of all things, look upon my misery with Thine eye of mercy, and let Thine infinite power vouchsafe to limit out some portion of deliverance unto me, as unto Thee shall seem most convenient. But yet, O my God, I yield unto Thy will, and joyfully embrace what sorrow Thou wilt have me suffer. Only thus much let me crave of Thee (let my craving, O Lord, be accepted of Thee, since even that proceeds from Thee)—let me crave even by the noblest title, which in my greatest affliction I may give myself, that I am Thy creature, and by Thy goodness (which is Thyself), that Thou wilt suffer some beam of Thy Majesty so to shine into my mind, that it may still depend confidently on Thee—Amen.

Sir Philip Sidney.

January the Thirty-first + + + + + 31

Oh, send Thy light and Thy truth, that I may live always near to Thee, my God. Oh, let me feel Thy love, that I may be, as it were, already in heaven, that I may do all my work as the angels do theirs; and Oh, let me be ready for every work! be ready to go out or go in, to stay or depart, just as Thou shalt appoint. Lord, let me have no will of my own; or consider my true happiness as depending, in the smallest degree, on anything that can befall me outwardly, but as consisting altogether in conformity to Thy will—Amen.

Henry Martyn (1781-1812).

God, Who chastisest us in Thy love, and refreshest us amid Thy chastening; grant that we may ever be able to give Thee thanks for both; through Jesus Christ our Lord—Amen.

Leonine Sacramentary, 440 A.D.

Forgive me my sins, O Lord, forgive me the sins of my youth and the sins of mine age, the sins of my soul, and the sins of my body, my secret and my whispering sins, my presumptuous and my crying sins, the sins that I have done to please myself, and the sins that I have done to please others. Forgive me those sins which I know, and those sins which I know not; forgive them, O Lord, forgive them all of Thy great goodness—Amen.

Private Devotions, 1560.

Grant, we beseech Thee, Almighty God, unto us who know that we are weak, and who trust in Thee because we know that Thou art strong, the gladsome help of Thy loving-kindness, both here in time and hereafter in eternity—Amen.

Roman Breviary.

February the Second ✢ ✢ ✢ ✢ ✢ ✢ 33

O God our heavenly Father, renew in us the sense of Thy gracious Presence, and let it be a constant impulse within us to peace, trustfulness, and courage on our pilgrimage. Let us hold Thee fast with a loving and adoring heart, and let our affections be fixed on Thee, that so the unbroken communion of our hearts with Thee may accompany us whatsoever we do, through life and in death. Teach us to pray heartily ; to listen for Thy voice within, and never to stifle its warnings. Behold, we bring our poor hearts as a sacrifice unto Thee : come and fill Thy sanctuary, and suffer nought impure to enter there. O Thou Who art Love, let Thy Divine Spirit flow like a river through our whole souls, and lead us in the right way till we pass by a peaceful death into the Land of Promise—Amen.

Gerhard Tersteegen.

February the Third

O Lord, begin, we beseech Thee, prosper and finish every good work whereunto Thou hast appointed us. Grant us grace here to do and suffer thankfully Thy most merciful Will, and hereafter to rejoice in Thy rest—Amen.

Christina G. Rossetti.

O Lord, Thou knowest what is best for us, let this or that be done, as Thou shalt please. Give what Thou wilt, and how much Thou wilt, and when Thou wilt. Deal with me as Thou thinkest good, and as best pleaseth Thee. Set me where Thou wilt, and deal with me in all things just as Thou wilt. Behold, I am Thy servant, prepared for all things; for I desire not to live unto myself, but unto Thee; and Oh, that I could do it worthily and perfectly!—Amen.

Thomas à Kempis.

February the Fourth ✦ ✦ ✦ ✦ ✦ ✦ 35

Teach me, O Lord, and enable me to live the life of saints and angels. Take me out of the languor, the irritability, the sensitiveness, the anarchy, in which my soul lies, and fill it with Thy fulness. Breathe on me with that Breath which infuses energy and kindles fervor. In asking for fervor, I ask for all that I can need, and all that Thou canst give. In asking for fervor, I am asking for faith, hope, and charity, in their most heavenly exercise; I am asking for that loyal perception of duty, which follows on yearning affection; I am asking for sanctity, peace, and joy, all at once. Nothing would be a trouble to me, nothing a difficulty, had I but fervor of soul. Lord, in asking for fervor, I am asking for Thyself, for nothing short of Thee, O my God. Enter my heart, and fill it with fervor by filling it with Thee—Amen.

John Henry Newman.

February the Fifth

Lord, Who, in infinite wisdom and love, orderest all things for Thy children, order everything this day for me in Thy tender pity. Thou knowest my weakness, Who madest me; Thou knowest how my soul shrinks from all pain of soul. Lord, I know Thou wilt lay no greater burden on me than Thou canst help me to bear. Teach me to receive all things this day from Thee. Enable me to commend myself in all things to Thee; grant me in all things to please Thee; bring me through all things nearer unto Thee; bring me, day by day, nearer to Thyself, to life everlasting—Amen.

E. B. Pusey.

Lord, make us, we implore Thee, so to love Thee that Thou mayest be to us a Fire of Love, purifying and not destroying—Amen.

Christina G. Rossetti.

February the Sixth + + + + + + + 37

Lord, give us hearts never to forget Thy love; but to dwell therein whatever we do, whether we sleep or wake, live or die, or rise again to the life that is to come. For Thy love is eternal life and everlasting rest; for this is life eternal to know Thee and Thy infinite goodness. O let its flame never be quenched in our hearts; let it grow and brighten, till our whole souls are glowing and shining with its light and warmth. Be Thou our Joy and Hope, our Strength and Life, our Shield and Shepherd, our Portion for ever. For happy are we if we continue in the love wherewith Thou hast loved us; holy are we when we love Thee steadfastly. Therefore O Thou, Whose name and essence is Love, enkindle our hearts, enlighten our understandings, sanctify our wills, and fill all the thoughts of our hearts, for Jesus Christ's sake—Amen.

Johann Arndt (1555-1621).

 Almighty God, give to Thy servant a meek and gentle spirit, that I may be slow to anger, and easy to mercy and forgiveness. Give me a wise and constant heart, that I may never be moved to an intemperate anger for any injury that is done or offered. Lord, let me ever be courteous, and easy to be entreated; let me never fall into a peevish or contentious spirit, but follow peace with all men; offering forgiveness inviting them by courtesies, ready to confess my own errors, apt to make amends, and desirous to be reconciled. Let no sickness or cross accident, no employment or weariness, make me angry or ungentle and discontented, or unthankful, or uneasy to them that minister to me; but in all things make me like unto the holy Jesus—Amen.

Jeremy Taylor.

February the Eighth ✦ ✦ ✦ ✦ ✦ ✦ 39

Preserve us blameless, O Lord, in our goings out and comings in this day. Fill us with the simplicity of a divine purpose, that we may be inwardly at one with Thy holy will, and lifted above vain wishes of our own. Set free from every detaining desire or reluctance, may we heartily surrender all our powers to the work which Thou hast given us to do; rejoicing in any toil, and fainting under no hardness that may befall us as good soldiers of Jesus Christ; and counting it as our crown of blessing if we may join the company of the faithful who have kept Thy Name and witnessed to Thy Kingdom in every age. Prepare us to seek our rest, not in outward ease, but in inward devotedness: only fulfil to us the word of the Chief of Saints; leave us His peace, while we remain here; and then receive us unto Thyself, to mingle with the mighty company of our forerunners—Amen.

James Martineau.

February the Ninth

O Lord, with Whom is the Fountain of Life, give us all, we entreat Thee, grace and good will to follow the leadings of Thy most Holy Spirit. Let the dew of Thy grace descend and abide upon us, refreshing that which droops, reviving that which is ready to perish ; until the day when all Thy faithful people shall drink of the river of Thy pleasures—Amen.

Christina G. Rossetti.

Eternal God, Who by Thy Holy breath of power makest us a new creation for Thyself, we beseech Thee to preserve what Thou hast created, and consecrate what Thou hast cleansed ; that by Thy grace we may be found in that form, the thought of which ever dwells with Thee, and which Thou willest fulfilled in man —Amen.

Rowland Williams.

February the Tenth ✦ ✦ ✦ ✦ ✦ ✦ ✦ 41

Be Thou present with me, O Lord, in every time and place. Let this be my consolation, to be cheerfully willing to do without all human comfort. And, if Thy consolation be wanting, let Thy will and just trial of me be unto me as the greatest comfort—Amen.

Thomas à Kempis.

Almighty God, the Refuge of all that are distressed, grant unto us that, in all trouble of this our mortal life, we may flee to the knowledge of Thy lovingkindness and tender mercy; that so, sheltering ourselves therein, the storms of life may pass over us, and not shake the peace of God that is within us. Whatsoever this life may bring us, grant that it may never take from us the full faith that Thou art our Father. Grant us Thy light, that we may have life, through Jesus Christ our Lord—Amen.

George Dawson.

Grant me, I beseech Thee, Almighty and most Merciful God, fervently to desire, wisely to search out, and perfectly to fulfil, all that is well-pleasing unto Thee. Order Thou my worldly condition to the glory of Thy name; and, of all that Thou requirest me to do, grant me the knowledge, the desire, and the ability, that I may so fulfil it as I ought, and may my path to Thee, I pray, be safe, straightforward, and perfect to the end.

Give me, O Lord, a steadfast heart, which no unworthy affection may drag downwards; give me an unconquered heart, which no tribulation can wear out; give me an upright heart, which no unworthy purpose may tempt aside.

Bestow upon me also, O Lord my God, understanding to know Thee, diligence to seek Thee, wisdom to find Thee, and a faithfulness that may finally embrace Thee—Amen.

St. Thomas Aquinas (1225-1274).

February the Twelfth ✦ ✦ ✦ ✦ ✦ ✦ 43

 Father, calm the turbulence of our passions; quiet the throbbing of our hopes; repress the waywardness of our wills; direct the motions of our affections; and sanctify the varieties of our lot. Be Thou all in all to us; and may all things earthly, while we bend them to our growth in grace, and to the work of blessing, dwell lightly in our hearts, so that we may readily, or even joyfully, give up whatever Thou dost ask for. May we seek first Thy kingdom and righteousness; resting assured that then all things needful shall be added unto us.

Father, pardon our past ingratitude and disobedience; and purify us, whether by Thy gentler or Thy sterner dealings, till we have done Thy will on earth, and Thou removest us to Thine own presence with the redeemed in heaven—Amen.

Mary Carpenter.

44 ✠ ✠ ✠ ✠ February the Thirteenth

Eternal Wisdom, grant me the light of Thy Holy Spirit, that I may know what Thou wouldest have me do; I offer myself entirely to Thee, do with me what seemeth good in Thy sight; not my will, but Thine, be done. Correct whatsoever Thou seest amiss in me, strengthen my weak resolutions, restrain my wayward desires; remove all hindrances to the fulfilment of Thy will, and give me grace so to follow the leadings of Thy Providence, that my life may be spent to Thy honor and glory, in whatsoever way it pleases Thee—Amen.

Treasury of Devotion.

Almighty God, we invoke Thee, the Fountain of everlasting Light; and entreat Thee to send forth Thy truth into our hearts, and to pour upon us the glory of Thy brightness, through Christ our Lord—Amen.

Sarum Breviary, A. D. 1085.

February the Fourteenth ✦ ✦ ✦ ✦ 45

O God, Who hast commanded that no man should be idle, give us grace to employ all our talents and faculties in the service appointed for us; that, whatsoever our hand findeth to do, we may do it with our might. Cheerfully may we go on in the road which Thou hast marked out, not desiring too earnestly that it should be either more smooth or more wide; but, daily seeking our way by Thy light, may we trust ourselves and the issue of our journey, to Thee the Fountain of Joy, and sing songs of praise as we go along. Then, O Lord, receive us at the gate of life which Thou hast opened for us in Christ Jesus—Amen.

Martineau's Common Prayer for Christian Worship.

February the Fifteenth

O Lord, we beseech Thee that Thy people may grow ever in love toward Thee, their Father Who art in heaven, and may so be schooled by holy works, that ever, as Thou dost pour Thy gifts upon them, they may walk before Thee in all such things as be well-pleasing in the sight of Thy Divine Majesty—Amen.

Roman Breviary.

Most loving Father, Who willest us to give thanks for all things, to dread nothing but the loss of Thee, and to cast all our care on Thee Who carest for us; preserve us from faithless fears and worldly anxieties, and grant that no clouds of this mortal life may hide from us the light of that Love which is immortal, and which Thou hast manifested unto us in Thy Son, Jesus Christ our Lord—Amen.

William Bright.

February the Sixteenth

Almighty God, Who alone gavest us the breath of life, and alone canst keep alive in us the breathing of holy desires, we beseech Thee for Thy compassions' sake to sanctify all our thoughts and endeavors, that we may neither begin any action without a pure intention, nor continue it without Thy blessing; and grant that, having the eyes of our understanding purged to behold things invisible and unseen, we may in heart be inspired with Thy wisdom, and in work be upheld by Thy strength, and in the end be accepted of Thee, as Thy faithful servants, having done all things to Thy glory, and thereby to our endless peace. Grant this prayer, O Lord—Amen.

Rowland Williams.

February the Seventeenth

Lord, Whom all Thy good creatures bless and praise according to Thy gift unto each of them, grant, we pray Thee, that we on whom Thou hast bestowed reason and speech may ever bless Thee with heart and lips, and may of Thine infinite mercy inherit a blessing, even the eternal blessedness of heaven—Amen.

Christina G. Rossetti.

Almighty and Everlasting God, Thou Lover of peace and concord, Who hast called us in Christ to love and unity: we pray Thee so rule our hearts by Thy Holy Spirit, that we, being delivered by the true fear of God from all fear of man, may evermore serve Thee in righteousness, mercy, humility, and gentleness towards each other, through Thy dear Son Jesus Christ our Lord—Amen.

Bunsen's Collection.

February the Eighteenth ✣ ✣ ✣ ✣ ✣

I Desire, O God, this day most earnestly to please Thee ; to do Thy will in each several thing which Thou shalt give me to do ; to bear each thing which Thou shalt allow to befall me contrary to my will, meekly, humbly, patiently, as a gift from Thee to subdue self-will in me ; and to make Thy will wholly mine. What I do, make me do, simply as Thy child ; let me be, throughout the day, as a child in his loving father's presence, ever looking up to Thee. May I love Thee for all Thy love. May I thank Thee, if not in words, yet in my heart, for each gift of Thy love, for each comfort which Thou allowest me day by day—Amen.

E. B. Pusey.

February the Nineteenth

O Heavenly Father, Who watchest always over Thy faithful people, and mightily defendest them, so that they be harmless preserved, I most heartily thank Thee, that it hath pleased Thy fatherly goodness to take care of me this night past. I most entirely beseech Thee, O most merciful Father, to show the like kindness toward me this day, in preserving my body and soul; that I may neither think, breathe, speak, or do anything that may be displeasing to Thy fatherly goodness, dangerous to myself, or hurtful to my neighbor; but that all my doings may be agreeable to Thy most blessed will, which is alway good; that they may advance Thy glory, answer to my vocation, and profit my neighbor, whom I ought to love as myself; that, whensoever Thou callest me hence, I may be found the child not of darkness but of light; through Jesus Christ our Lord—Amen.

Thomas Becon (1511–1570).

February the Twentieth + + + + + 51

Grant unto us, Almighty God, that we, communing with one another and with Thee, may feel our hearts burn within us, until all pure, and just, and holy, and noble things of God and man may be to us lovely, and we may find nothing to fear but that which is hateful in Thine eyes, and nothing worth seeking but that which is lovely and fair therein. Let the divine brightness and peace possess our souls, so that, fearing neither life nor death, we may look to Thy lovingkindness and tender mercy to lift us above that which is low and mean within us, and at last to give the spirit within us the victory, and bring us safe through death into the life everlasting. Hear us of Thy mercy, through Jesus Christ our Lord—Amen.

George Dawson.

O Thou Good Omnipotent, Who so carest for every one of us, as if Thou caredst for him alone; and so for all, as if all were but one! Blessed is the man who loveth Thee, and his friend in Thee, and his enemy for Thee. For he only loses none dear to him, to whom all are dear in Him who cannot be lost. And who is that but our God, the God that made heaven and earth, and filleth them, even by filling them creating them. And Thy law is truth, and truth is Thyself. I behold how some things pass away that others may replace them, but Thou dost never depart, O God, my Father supremely good, Beauty of all things beautiful. To Thee will I intrust whatsoever I have received from Thee, so shall I lose nothing. Thou madest me for Thyself, and my heart is restless until it repose in Thee—Amen.

St. Augustine (354-430).

February the Twenty-second +++ 53

With all my heart and soul, O God, I thank Thee, that in all the changes and chances of this mortal life, I can look up to Thee, and cheerfully resign my will to Thine. I have trusted Thee, O Father, with myself; my soul is in Thy hand, which I verily believe Thou wilt preserve from all evil; my body, and all that belongs to it, are of much less value. I do therefore, with as great security as satisfaction, trust all I have to Thee. I am persuaded that neither tribulation, nor anguish, nor persecution, nor famine, nor nakedness, nor peril, nor sword, nor death which I may fear, nor life which I may hope for, nor things present which I feel, nor things to come which I may apprehend, shall ever prevail so far over me, as to make me not to resign my will entirely to Thee—Amen.

Thomas Wilson (1663-1755).

February the Twenty-third

O God, we have known and believed the love that Thou hast for us. May we, by dwelling in love, dwell in Thee, and Thou in us. May we learn to love Thee Whom we have not seen, by loving our brethren whom we have seen. Teach us, O heavenly Father, the love wherewith Thou hast loved us; fashion us, O blessed Lord, after Thine own example of love; shed abroad, O Thou Holy Spirit of Love, the love of God and man in our hearts— Amen.

Henry Alford.

O Lord, vouchsafe to look mercifully upon us, and grant that we may choose the way of peace; so that, rescued from the captivity of the sins which have oppressed us, we may attain the dwellings of the heavenly Jerusalem; through Jesus Christ— Amen.

Sarum Breviary, A. D. 1085.

February the Twenty-fourth ✢ ✢ ✢ 55

Lord our God, teach us, we beseech Thee, to ask Thee aright for the right blessings. Steer Thou the vessel of our life toward Thyself, Thou tranquil Haven of all storm-tossed souls. Show us the course wherein we should go. Renew a willing spirit within us. Let Thy Spirit curb our wayward senses, and guide and enable us unto that which is our true good, to keep Thy laws, and in all our works evermore to rejoice in Thy glorious and gladdening Presence. For Thine is the glory and praise from all Thy saints for ever and ever—Amen.

St. Basil, A. D. 379

Lord, our Refuge from the storm, hide us, we entreat Thee, in Thine own Presence from the provoking of all men. By Thy holy love and fear, keep us from sins of temper and of the tongue—Amen.

Christina G. Rossetti.

May we lift our hearts to Thee this day in great thankfulness, humbly acknowledging Thy mercy and Thy truth, Thy large and tender providence, Thy nearness to us at all times, Thy Spirit of Wisdom and Might and Peace, the works and the joys and the discipline of earth which Thou dost appoint, the promises that lay hold of things to come. O Spirit of all grace and benediction, Father of our dear Lord and Saviour, coming to us in Him and in His, Creator of these dying bodies, Life and Light of these undying souls, Thy gifts are new upon us every morning. May Thy great love redeem us; and from the light of a true life below may we pass at length into that Presence where there is fullness of joy and abundance of peace forever—Amen.

Rufus Ellis.

February the Twenty-sixth + + + 57

**Lord, my God, Light of the** blind and Strength of the weak; yea, also, Light of those that see, and Strength of the strong; hearken unto my soul, and hear it crying out of the depths.

O Lord, help us to turn and seek Thee; for Thou hast not forsaken Thy creatures as we have forsaken Thee, our Creator. Let us turn and seek Thee, for we know Thou art here in our hearts, when we confess to Thee, when we cast ourselves upon Thee, and weep in Thy bosom, after all our rugged ways; and Thou dost gently wipe away our tears, and we weep the more for joy; because Thou, Lord, who madest us, dost remake and comfort us.

Hear, Lord, my prayer, and grant that I may most entirely love Thee, and do Thou rescue me, O Lord, from every temptation, even unto the end—Amen.

St. Augustine (354-430).

58 ✢ ✢ February the Twenty-seventh

O Lord, make Thy law, I entreat Thee, our delight. Plant in our hearts love which is the fulfilling of the law. Teach us to love Thee with our whole will and being, and our neighbor as ourselves. Keep us from dividing Thy commandments into great and small, according to our own blind estimate; but give us grace humbly to acknowledge that whoso transgresseth in one point is guilty of the whole law—Amen.

Christina G. Rossetti.

Guide me, O Lord, in all the changes and varieties of the world; that in all things that shall happen, I may have an evenness and tranquillity of spirit; that my soul may be wholly resigned to Thy divinest will and pleasure, never murmuring at Thy gentle chastisements and fatherly correction—Amen.

Jeremy Taylor.

February the Twenty-eighth + + + 59

Grant us grace to rest from all sinful deeds and thoughts, to surrender ourselves wholly unto Thee, and to keep our souls still before Thee like a still lake; that so the beams of Thy grace may be mirrored therein, and may kindle in our hearts the glow of faith and love and prayer. May we, through such stillness and hope, find strength and gladness in Thee, O God, now and forever more—Amen.

    Joachim Embden (1595-1650).

So fill us with Thy Spirit, O Lord, that we, passing from one thing to another, may go from strength to strength; everywhere full of Thy praise, everywhere full of Thy work, finding the joy of the Lord to be our strength, until the time when the work of this world shall close, and the weary hours shall come to an end, and darkness shall come, and our eyes shall rest for a while; then give us an abundant entrance into the life eternal, through Jesus Christ our Lord—Amen.

    George Dawson.

60 ✣ ✣ ✣ February the Twenty-ninth

Give me, O Lord, purity of lips, a clean and innocent heart, humility, fortitude, patience. Give me the Spirit of wisdom and understanding, the Spirit of counsel and strength, the Spirit of knowledge and godliness, and of Thy fear. Make me ever to seek Thy face with all my heart, all my soul, all my mind; grant me to have a contrite and humble heart in Thy presence. Most high, eternal, and ineffable Wisdom, drive away from me the darkness of blindness and ignorance; most high and eternal Strength, deliver me; most high and eternal Light, illuminate me; most high and infinite Mercy, have mercy on me—Amen.

Gallican Sacramentary, A. D. 800.

Lord, give us the grace of Thy Spirit, early to seek out, and evermore earnestly to follow the work which Thou hast appointed for us to do—Amen.

Henry Alford.

March the First

O Holy Spirit, Love of God, infuse Thy grace, and descend plentifully into my heart; enlighten the dark corners of this neglected dwelling, and scatter there Thy cheerful beams; dwell in that soul that longs to be Thy temple; water that barren soil, over-run with weeds and briars, and lost for want of cultivating, and make it fruitful with Thy dew from heaven. Oh come, Thou refreshment of them that languish and faint. Come, Thou Star and Guide of them that sail in the tempestuous sea of the world; Thou only Haven of the tossed and shipwrecked. Come, Thou Glory and Crown of the living, and only Safeguard of the dying. Come, Holy Spirit, in much mercy, and make me fit to receive Thee—Amen.

St. Augustine (354-430).

Hear us, O never-failing Light, Lord our God, the Fountain of light, the Light of Thine Angels, Principalities, Powers, and of all intelligent beings; who hast created the light of Thy Saints. May our souls be lamps of Thine, kindled and illuminated by Thee. May they shine and burn with the truth, and never go out in darkness and ashes. May the gloom of sins be cleared away, and the light of perpetual faith abide within us—Amen.

Mozarabic, before A. D. 700.

O God, the Sovereign Good of the soul, who requirest the hearts of all Thy children; deliver us from all sloth in Thy work, all coldness in Thy cause; and grant us by looking unto Thee to rekindle our love, and by waiting upon Thee to renew our strength, through Jesus Christ our Lord —Amen.

William Bright.

March the Third ✢ ✢ ✢ ✢ ✢ ✢ ✢ ✢ ✢ 63

 **O God, Gracious and Merciful,** give us, we entreat Thee, a humble trust in Thy mercy, and suffer not our heart to fail us. Though our sins be seven, though our sins be seventy times seven, though our sins be more in number than the hairs of our head, yet give us grace in loving penitence to cast ourselves down into the depth of Thy compassion—Amen.

Christina G. Rossetti.

 **O God, the Source of perfect** blessedness, who dost teach Thy faithful ones to walk in Thy laws, to search Thy testimonies, to keep Thy commands; grant unto us, we beseech Thee, Thy righteousness, that we may seek Thee with our whole hearts; that we, who hitherto have wandered like lost sheep, restored by Thy kind arms, may rejoice in the glories of Paradise, through Jesus Christ Thy Son ‑ —Amen.

Sarum Breviary, A.D. 1085.

I Will say unto my God, my Lord, and my King, "O how great is the abundance of Thy goodness, O Lord, which Thou hast laid up for them that fear Thee." But what art Thou to those who love Thee? What to those who serve Thee with their whole heart? In this especially Thou hast showed me the sweetness of Thy love; that, when I was not, Thou madest me, when I went far astray from Thee, Thou broughtest me back again, that I might serve Thee, and hast commanded me to love Thee. I would I were able, at least for one day, to do Thee some worthy service. Truly, Thou art my Lord, and I Thy servant, who am bound to serve Thee with all my might; and this I wish to do, this I desire; and whatsoever is wanting unto me, do Thou, I beseech Thee, vouchsafe to supply—Amen.

Thomas a Kempis.

March the Fifth ✛ ✛ ✛ ✛ ✛ ✛ ✛ ✛ 65

Infinite and Holy One, whom we know as our Father and the Father of our Lord Jesus Christ, we devoutly thank Thee for the mercy that created us from the dust, and for the greater mercy that has created us anew by a heavenly adoption as Thy children. For the undying yearnings, which Thou hast implanted in us, after things unseen,—for their satisfaction in Thyself, we thank Thee; and we rejoice that Thou hast been willing to encourage our frail and mortal spirits, by revealing to us something of the perfections of Thy nature, and calling us to follow after Thee. Grant, we pray, that Thy loving-kindness may be followed by our obedience. And do Thou so confirm our best purposes by renewing our sense of Thy presence, that we may both imitate Thy nature, and accept Thy dealings with us in the spirit of childlike trust, and by the help of Thy dear Son, Jesus Christ our Lord—Amen.

Henry W. Foote.

O Lord, the Portion of our inheritance, give us grace, I pray Thee, never to aim at or desire anything out of Thee. What we can enjoy in Thee, give us according to Thy will; what we cannot, deny us —Amen.

Christina G. Rossetti.

Grant unto us, O Lord God, that we may love one another unfeignedly; for where love is, there art Thou; and he that loveth his brother is born of Thee, and dwelleth in Thee, and Thou in him. And where brethren do glorify Thee with one accord, there dost Thou pour out Thy blessing upon them. Love us, therefore, O Lord, and shed Thy love into our hearts, that we may love Thee, and our brethren in Thee and for Thee, as all children to Thee, through Jesus Christ our Lord—Amen.

A. D. 1578.

March the Seventh · · · · · · · 67

Lord, hear; Lord, forgive; Lord, do; hear what I speak not, forgive what I speak amiss, do what I leave undone; that, not according to my word or my deed, but according to Thy mercy and truth, all may issue to Thy glory and the good of Thy kingdom—Amen.

Maria Hare.

Almighty and Eternal God, who hast revealed Thy nature in Christ Jesus Thy Son as Love: we humbly pray Thee give us Thy Holy Spirit, to glorify Thee also in our hearts as pure Love, and thus constrain us by Thy Divine power to love Thee again with our whole souls, and our brethren as ourselves; that so by Thy grace we may be fulfilled with love, and evermore abide in Thee and Thou in us, with all joyfulness, and free from fear or distrust, through Jesus Christ our Lord—Amen.

Bunsen's Collection.

We bless and praise and magnify Thee, O God of our fathers, who hast led us out of the shadows of night once more into the light of day. Unto Thy loving-kindness we make our entreaty; be merciful to our misdeeds; accept our prayers in the fulness of Thy compassions, for Thou art our refuge from one generation to another, O merciful and almighty God. Suffer the true Sun of Thy righteousness to shine in our hearts, enlighten our reason, and purify our senses; that so we may walk honestly as in the day, in the way of Thy commandments, and reach at last the life eternal, where we shall rejoice in Thy inaccessible life. For Thou art the Fountain of Life, and in Thy light shall we see light—Amen.

Greek Church.

Searcher of hearts, Thou knowest us better than we know ourselves, and seest the sins which our sinfulness hides from us. Yet even our own conscience beareth witness against us, that we often slumber on our appointed watch; that we walk not always lovingly with each other, and humbly with Thee; and we withhold that entire sacrifice of ourselves to Thy perfect will, without which we are not crucified with Christ, or sharers in His redemption. Oh, look upon our contrition, and lift up our weakness, and let the dayspring yet arise within our hearts, and bring us healing, strength, and joy. Day by day may we grow in faith, in self-denial, in charity, in heavenly-mindedness. And then, mingle us at last with the mighty host of Thy redeemed for evermore—Amen.

James Martineau.

March the Tenth

O Lord, perfect, we beseech Thee, the faith of us who believe, and sow the good seed of faith in their hearts who as yet lack it; that we all may look steadfastly unto Thee, and run with patience the race that is set before us. Give us grace to show our faith by our works; teach us to walk by faith, having respect unto the promises: which of Thy mercy make good to us in Thine own good time, O our most Gracious Lord God and Saviour—Amen.

Christina G. Rossetti.

Lord, let Thy holy breath ever keep alive in us that fire which Thy Son of old came to kindle upon earth, that we also may be anointed with the spirit of peace, holiness, and obedience, and dwell in Thy fellowship for ever—Amen.

Rowland Williams.

March the Eleventh ✦ ✦ ✦ ✦ ✦ ✦ 71

O God, who seest all our weaknesses, and the troubles we labor under, have regard unto the prayers of Thy servant, who stands in need of Thy comfort, Thy direction, and Thy help. Thou alone knowest what is best for us; let me never dispute Thy wisdom or Thy goodness. Lord, so prepare my heart, that no affliction may ever so surprise as to overbear me. Dispose me at all times to a readiness to suffer what Thy Providence shall order or permit. Grant that I may never murmur at Thy appointments, nor be exasperated at the ministers of Thy Providence—Amen.

Thomas Wilson (1663-1755).

✦

Feed Thy people, O Lord, with Thy grace, and deliver our souls from the death of sin; so that, being filled with Thy mercy, we may be united with the joys of the righteous, through Jesus Christ our Lord—Amen.

Sarum Breviary, A. D. 1085.

March the Twelfth

 My Father, I have moments of deep unrest—moments when I know not what to ask by reason of the very excess of my wants. I have in these hours no words for Thee, no conscious prayers for Thee. My cry seems purely worldly; I want only the wings of a dove that I may flee away. Yet all the time Thou hast accepted my unrest as a prayer. Thou hast interpreted its cry for a dove's wings as a cry for Thee, Thou hast received the nameless longings of my heart as the intercessions of Thy Spirit. They are not yet the intercessions of my spirit; I know not what I ask. But Thou knowest what I ask, O my God. Thou knowest the name of that need which lies beneath my speechless groan. Thou knowest that, because I am made in Thine image, I can find rest only in what gives rest to Thee; therefore Thou hast counted my unrest unto me for righteousness, and hast called my groaning Thy Spirit's prayer—Amen.

George Matheson.

March the Thirteenth ✢ ✢ ✢ ✢ ✢ ✢ 73

Ah, Lord God, Thou holy Lover of my soul, when Thou comest into my soul, all that is within me shall rejoice. Thou art my Glory and the exultation of my heart; Thou art my Hope and Refuge in the day of my trouble. Set me free from all evil passions, and heal my heart of all inordinate affections; that, being inwardly cured and thoroughly cleansed, I may be made fit to love, courageous to suffer, steady to persevere. Nothing is sweeter than Love, nothing more courageous, nothing fuller nor better in heaven and earth; because Love is born of God, and cannot rest but in God, above all created things. Let me love Thee more than myself, nor love myself but for Thee; and in Thee all that truly love Thee, as the law of Love commandeth, shining out from Thyself—Amen.

Thomas a Kempis.

Teach me, O Father, how to ask Thee each moment, silently, for Thy help. If I fail, teach me at once to ask Thee to forgive me. If I am disquieted, enable me, by Thy grace, quickly to turn to Thee. May nothing this day come between me and Thee. May I will, do, and say, just what Thou, my loving and tender Father, willest me to will, do, and say. Work Thy holy will in me and through me this day. Protect me, guide me, bless me, within and without, that I may do something this day for love of Thee; something which shall please Thee; and that I may, this evening, be nearer to Thee, though I see it not, nor know it. Lead me, O Lord, in a straight way unto Thyself, and keep me in Thy grace unto the end—Amen.

E. B. Pusey.

March the Fifteenth ✦ ✦ ✦ ✦ ✦ ✦ ✦ 75

I know, O Lord, and do with all humility acknowledge myself an object altogether unworthy of Thy love; but sure I am, Thou art an object altogether worthy of mine. I am not good enough to serve Thee, but Thou hast a right to the best service I can pay. Do Thou then impart to me some of that excellence, and that shall supply my own want of worth. Help me to cease from sin according to Thy will, that I may be capable of doing Thee service according to my duty. Enable me so to guard and govern myself, so to begin and finish my course, that, when the race of life is run, I may sleep in peace, and rest in Thee. Be with me unto the end, that my sleep may be rest indeed, my rest perfect security, and that security a blessed eternity—Amen.

St. Augustine (354-430).

Rest upon us, O Spirit of Love, and chase all anger, envy, and bitter grudges from our souls. Be our Comforter in trial, when the billows go over our heads; be our Strength in the hour of weakness, and help us to control the desires of the flesh. Let us grow in faith and love, in hope, patience, and humility. See by how many temptations we are surrounded, and preserve us from giving way to them; show us the path wherein we should tread, for if we trust to our own impulses we shall go astray; but if Thou lead us we shall run in the way of Thy commandments. Our hearts lie open before Thee; enter now with Thy rich gifts, strengthen, stablish, settle them. Dwell in them and make them Thy temple, so shall we have the pledge of our sonship, and of our salvation—Amen.

J. F. Stark (1680-1756).

March the Seventeenth ✦ ✦ ✦ ✦ ✦ 77

Merciful God, full of compassion, long-suffering and of great pity, make me earnestly repent, and heartily to be sorry for all my misdoings; make the remembrance of them so burdensome and painful that I may flee to Thee with a troubled spirit and a contrite heart; and, O merciful Lord, visit, comfort, and relieve me; excite in me true repentance; give me in this world knowledge of Thy truth and confidence in Thy mercy, and, in the world to come, life everlasting. Strengthen me against sin, and enable me so to perform every duty, that whilst I live I may serve Thee in that state to which Thou hast called me; and, at last, by a holy and happy death, be delivered from the struggles and sorrows of this life, and obtain eternal happiness, for the sake of our Lord and Saviour, Thy Son Jesus Christ—Amen.

     Samuel Johnson (1709-1784).

March the Eighteenth

Thou Hope of all the ends of the earth; Thou on whom our fathers hoped, and were not confounded; Thou, who knowest whereof we are made, and whereby our shortcoming, have pity on us, O Lord. O Helper of the helpless, and Stronger than the strong, remember all who are in distress of mind, body, or estate; succor them according to their need. It is meet and right, in all things, for all men, in joy and sorrow, alone and all together, to remember and worship Thee, to trust in Thee, and praise Thee, Lord and Father, King and God, Fountain of life and immortality, Source of everlasting good. Thee all the heavens hymn, and higher spirits praise, crying to each other, or going on the work which Thou givest them, and so perfecting praise. Blessed be the Dweller of Eternity, my Strength and my Deliverer, my Salvation and my Refuge for ever— Amen.

Rowland Williams.

March the Nineteenth ✦ ✦ ✦ ✦ ✦ 79

Most merciful and gracious Father, I bless and magnify Thy name that Thou hast adopted me into the inheritance of sons, and hast given me a portion of my elder Brother. Thou who art the God of patience and consolation, strengthen me that I may bear the yoke and burden, of the Lord, without any uneasy and useless murmurs, and ineffective unwillingness. Lord, I am unable to stand under the cross, unable of myself, but be Thou pleased to ease this load by fortifying my spirit, that I may be strongest when I am weakest, and may be able to do and suffer every thing that Thou pleasest, through Christ who strengtheneth me. Let me pass through the valley of tears, and the valley of the shadow of death with safety and peace, with a meek spirit, and a sense of the divine mercies. through Jesus Christ—Amen.

Jeremy Taylor (1613-1667).

March the Twentieth

Guide us in Thy way, O Lord, and mercifully show the fountain of wisdom to our thirsting minds; that we may be free from sorrowful heaviness, and may drink in the sweetness of life eternal—Amen.

Mozarabic, before A. D. 700.

I need Thee to teach me day by day, according to each day's opportunities and needs. Give me, O my Lord, that purity of conscience which alone can receive, which alone can improve Thy inspirations. My ears are dull, so that I cannot hear Thy voice. My eyes are dim, so that I cannot see Thy tokens. Thou alone canst quicken my hearing, and purge my sight, and cleanse and renew my heart. Teach me to sit at Thy feet, and to hear Thy word—Amen.

John Henry Newman.

March the Twenty-first ✢ ✢ ✢ ✢ ✢ 81

**God of Light, Father of Life,** Giver of Wisdom, Benefactor of our souls, who givest to the faint-hearted who put their trust in Thee those things into which the angels desire to look ; O Sovereign Lord, who hast brought us up from the depths of darkness to light, who hast given us life from death, who hast graciously bestowed upon us freedom from slavery, and who hast scattered the darkness of sin within us ; do Thou now also enlighten the eyes of our understanding, and sanctify us wholly in soul, body, and spirit—Amen.

Liturgy of St. Mark (175-254?).

**Lord, give us all, we beseech** Thee, grace and strength to overcome every sin ; sins of besetment, deliberation, surprise, negligence, omission ; sins against Thee, our self, our neighbor ; sins great, small, remembered, forgotten—Amen.

Christina G. Rossetti.

March the Twenty-second

My adorable God, I humbly beseech Thee to accept the sacrifice I here, in all humility, desire to make Thee, of the remainder of my life; to be entirely employed, with the utmost vigor both of my soul and body, in Thy service and adoration. Pardon all the sins and offences of my life past, and be pleased to bestow upon me a steadfast faith, an ardent love, an humble and perfect obedience, and a will capable of no other inclination than what it shall continually receive from the absolute guidance of Thy divine will; to which I beg it may be ever perfectly subservient, with all readiness and cheerfulness. As all my thoughts and actions are continually before Thee, so I humbly beseech Thee, that they may never be unworthy of Thy divine Presence, for Jesus Christ's sake—Amen.

Charles How (1661-1745).

March the Twenty-third

O God, ever blessed and holy! none but the angels and Thy redeemed can serve Thee with a perfect joy. Called in our measure to be perfect as Thou art perfect, we have been most unlike to Thee, and are not worthy to be deemed Thy children. Thirsting with momentary desires, we have forsaken the living springs of heavenly wisdom, of which he that drinketh shall never thirst again. We have been slow to the calls of affection, heedless of the duties, hard under the sorrows, which are Thy gracious discipline; yet are oppressed with cares Thou layest not on us, with ease Thou dost not permit, and wants Thou wilt never bless. Visit us with the wrestlings of Thy Spirit: and lay on us the cross, if we may but grow into the holiness, of Christ—Amen.

James Martineau.

84 ✢ ✢ ✢ ✢ March the Twenty-fourth

Almighty God, of Thy fulness grant to us who need so much, who lack so much, who have so little, wisdom and strength. Bring our wills unto Thine. Lift our understandings into Thy heavenly light; that we thereby beholding those things which are right, and being drawn by Thy love, may bring our will and our understanding together to Thy service, until at last, body and soul and spirit may be all Thine, and Thou be our Father and our Eternal Friend—Amen.

George Dawson.

Almighty God, who seest that we have no power of ourselves to help ourselves, keep us both outwardly in our bodies and inwardly in our souls, that we may be defended from all adversities which may happen to the body, and from all evil thoughts which may assault and hurt the soul; through Jesus Christ our Lord—Amen.

Gregorian, A.D. 590.

March the Twenty-fifth ✦ ✦ ✦ ✦ ✦ 85

Eternal Purity! Thou art brighter than the sun, purer than the angels, and the heavens are not clean in Thy sight; with mercy behold Thy servant, apt to be tempted with every object, and to be overcome by every enemy. I cannot, O God, stand in the day of battle and danger, unless Thou coverest me with Thy shield, and hidest me under Thy wings. Thou didst make me after Thine image; be pleased to preserve me so pure and spotless, that my body may be a holy temple, and my soul a sanctuary to entertain Thy divinest Spirit, the Spirit of love and holiness—Amen.

Jeremy Taylor (1613-1667).

O God, deliver us from earthly desires, that no sin may reign in us, but that we may with free spirits serve Thee, our only Lord; through Jesus Christ—Amen.

Gelasian Sacramentary, A. D. 492.

March the Twenty-sixth

O Lord, give Thy blessing, we pray Thee, to our daily work, that we may do it in faith and heartily, as to the Lord and not unto men. All our powers of body and mind are Thine, and we would fain devote them to Thy service. Sanctify them, and the work in which they are engaged; let us not be slothful, but fervent in spirit, and do Thou, O Lord, so bless our efforts that they may bring forth in us the fruits of true wisdom. Teach us to seek after truth and enable us to gain it; but grant that we may ever speak the truth in love; that, while we know earthly things, we may know Thee, and be known by Thee, through and in Thy Son Jesus Christ. Give us this day Thy Holy Spirit, that we may be Thine in body and spirit in all our work and all our refreshments, through Jesus Christ Thy Son, our Lord—Amen.

Thomas Arnold.

March the Twenty-seventh ✦ ✦ ✦ 87

Oh Thou gracious and gentle and condescending God, Thou God of peace, Father of mercy, God of all comfort; see, I lament before Thee the evil of my heart; I acknowledge that I am too much disposed to anger, jealousy, and revenge, to ambition and pride, which often give rise to discord and bitter feelings between me and others. Too often have I thus offended and grieved both Thee, O long-suffering Father, and my fellow-men. Oh forgive me this sin, and suffer me to partake of the blessing which Thou hast promised to the peacemakers, who shall be called the children of God.

Bestow on me, O Lord, a genial spirit and unwearied forbearance; a mild, loving, patient heart; kindly looks, pleasant, cordial speech and manners in the intercourse of daily life; that I may give offence to none, but as much as in me lies live in charity with all men—Amen.

Johann Arndt (1555-1621).

March the Twenty-eighth

God, my God, I am all weakness, but Thou art my Strength; I am ever anew bowed down by any trial, but Thou canst and willest to lift me up. Let me not fail, O God my Strength; let me not be discouraged, O God, my Hope. Draw me each day, if it be but a little nearer unto Thee; make me, each day, if it be but a little less unlike Thee; let me do or bear each day something, for love of Thee, whereby I may be fitter for Thee. Let no day pass without my having done something pleasing unto Thee. Thus alone would I live, that I may live more unto Thee; thus would I die, longing to love Thee more—Amen.   E. B. Pusey.

God, the Shepherd of all Thy people, deliver the same from all sins which do assail them, that so they may ever be pleasing in Thy sight, and safe under Thy shelter; for Christ's sake—Amen.

Roman Breviary.

March the Twenty-ninth ✧ ✧ ✧ ✧ 89

Thou who chastenest whom Thou lovest, grant us grace, we pray Thee, to discern Thy love in whatever suffering Thou sendest us. Support us in patient thankfulness under pain, anxiety, or loss, and move us with pity and tenderness for our afflicted neighbors—Amen.

Christina G. Rossetti.

Lord, let me not henceforth desire health or life, except to spend them for Thee, with Thee, and in Thee. Thou alone knowest what is good for me; do, therefore, what seemeth Thee best. Give to me, or take from me; conform my will to Thine; and grant that, with humble and perfect submission, and in holy confidence, I may receive the orders of Thine eternal Providence; and may equally adore all that comes to me from Thee; through Jesus Christ our Lord—Amen.

Blaise Pascal (1623-1662).

**O Lord, succor, we beseech Thee,** us who are tempted. May nothing induce us to distrust Thy care over us, nor to use Thy gifts to the denial of Thee, their Giver. May we never presume upon Thy protection when we are forsaking Thy paths, and tempting Thee. May we never, for the sake of any supposed gain or advancement, quench the testimony of Thy Spirit, or prove disloyal to Thy service. Do Thou so support us in all temptations that, when we have been tried, we may receive the crown of life, which Thou hast prepared for them that love Thee—Amen.

Henry Alford.

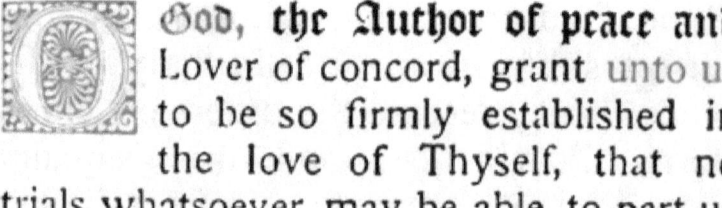**O God, the Author of peace and** Lover of concord, grant unto us to be so firmly established in the love of Thyself, that no trials whatsoever may be able to part us from Thee—Amen.

Roman Breviary.

March the Thirty-first

We beseech Thee, O Lord, make us subject unto Thee with a ready will, and evermore stir up our wills to make supplication unto Thee—Amen.

Gelasian, A. D. 492.

Almighty God, Maker of heaven and earth, Giver of light and life, so teach us those things which belong to the heavenly kingdom, and those duties which are of the earth, that we, stirred by the light and life of the peace of God, may be enabled faithfully to do the things committed to us, looking ever unto Thee for light and life, that, being lifted above ourselves, the life of God in the soul of man may be ours, and the peace of God, which passeth all understanding, may then keep our hearts and minds, through Jesus Christ our Lord—Amen.

George Dawson.

O Lord, whose way is perfect, help us, I pray Thee, always to trust in Thy goodness: that walking with Thee and following Thee in all simplicity, we may possess quiet and contented minds; and may cast all our care on Thee, for Thou carest for us—Amen.

Christina G. Rossetti.

O Lord, if only my will may remain right and firm towards Thee, do with me whatsoever it shall please Thee. For it cannot be anything but good, whatsoever Thou shalt do with me. If it be Thy will I should be in darkness, be Thou blessed; and if it be Thy will I should be in light, be Thou again blessed. If Thou vouchsafe to comfort me, be Thou blessed; and, if Thou wilt have me afflicted, be Thou ever equally blessed—Amen.

Thomas à Kempis.

April the Second ✛ ✛ ✛ ✛ ✛ ✛ ✛ 93

Eternal God, who committest to us the swift and solemn trust of life; since we know not what a day may bring forth, but only that the hour for serving Thee is always present, may we wake to the instant claims of Thy holy will; not waiting for to-morrow, but yielding to-day. Lay to rest, by the persuasion of Thy Spirit, the resistance of our passion, indolence or fear. Consecrate with Thy presence the way our feet may go; and the humblest work will shine, and the roughest places be made plain. Lift us above unrighteous anger and mistrust into faith and hope and charity by a simple and steadfast reliance on Thy sure will. In all things draw us to the mind of Christ, that Thy lost image may be traced again, and Thou mayest own us as at one with Him and Thee—Amen.

James Martineau.

April the Third

O Most dear and tender Father, our Defender and Nourisher; endue us with Thy grace, that we may cast off the great blindness of our minds, and carefulness of worldly things, and may put our whole study and care in keeping of Thy holy law; and that we may labor and travail for our necessities in this life, like the birds of the air and the lilies of the field, without care. For Thou hast promised to be careful for us; and hast commanded that upon Thee we should cast our care, who livest and reignest, world without end—Amen.

Henry VIII's Primer, 1545.

Lord, fill us, we beseech Thee, with adoring gratitude to Thee for all Thou art for us, to us, and in us; fill us with love, joy, peace, and all the fruits of the Spirit—Amen.

Christina G. Rossetti.

April the Fourth ✦ ✦ ✦ ✦ ✦ ✦ ✦ ✦ 95

The day returns and brings us the petty round of irritating concerns and duties. Help us to play the man, help us to perform them with laughter and kind faces, let cheerfulness abound with industry. Give us to go blithely on our business all this day, bring us to our resting beds weary and content and undishonored, and grant us in the end the gift of sleep—Amen.

R. L. Stevenson.

O God, who through the grace of Thy Holy Spirit, dost pour the gift of love into the hearts of Thy faithful people, grant unto us health, both of mind and body, that we may love Thee with our whole strength, and with entire satisfaction may perform those things which are pleasing unto Thee, through Christ our Lord—Amen.

Sarum Breviary, A. D. 1085.

April the Fifth

Grant, gracious Father, that I may never dispute the reasonableness of Thy will, but ever close with it, as the best that can happen. Prepare me always for what Thy Providence shall bring forth. Let me never murmur, be dejected, or impatient, under any of the troubles of this life, but ever find rest and comfort in this, THIS IS THE WILL OF MY FATHER, AND OF MY GOD: grant this for Jesus Christ's sake—Amen.

Thomas Wilson (1663-1755).

O God, the Consolation of all such as be sorrowful, and the Salvation of all them that put their trust in Thee, grant unto us, in this dying life, that peace for which we humbly pray, and hereafter to attain unto everlasting joy in Thy presence, through our Lord Jesus Christ—Amen.

Roman Breviary.

April the Sixth ✢ ✢ ✢ ✢ ✢ ✢ ✢ ✢ ✢ ✢ 97

 **Lord, make us to love Thee,** and each other in Thee, and to meet before Thee to dwell in Thine everlasting love—Amen.

E. B. Pusey.

Grant unto us, Almighty God, the knowledge of Thy way, and the spirit of obedience thereunto, that, being conformed in thought and words unto Thy way, Thy peace may rule in our hearts. Help us to cast out all those things which are contrary to Thy peace, or that are not according to Thy will, that so ours may be the quiet life of trust, and faith, and obedience, living lowly, longing for Thy truth, and walking in the light thereof, that Thy blessing may be upon us, and the light of Thy countenance our perpetual delight. Hear us of Thy mercy, through Jesus Christ our Lord—Amen.

George Dawson.

We most earnestly beseech Thee, O Thou Lover of mankind, to bless all Thy people, the flocks of Thy fold. Send down into our hearts the peace of heaven, and grant us also the peace of this life. Give life to the souls of all of us, and let no deadly sin prevail against us, or any of Thy people. Deliver all who are in trouble, for Thou art our God, who settest the captives free; who givest hope to the hopeless, and help to the helpless; who liftest up the fallen; and who art the Haven of the shipwrecked. Give Thy pity, pardon, and refreshment to every Christian soul, whether in affliction or error. Preserve us, in our pilgrimage through this life from hurt and danger, and grant that we may end our lives as Christians, well-pleasing to Thee and free from sin, and that we may have our portion and lot with all Thy saints—Amen.

Liturgy of St. Mark (175–254?).

April the Eighth ✛ ✛ ✛ ✛ ✛ ✛ ✛ ✛ 99

Give us grace, O Lord, to work while it is day, fulfilling diligently and patiently whatever duty Thou appointest us; doing small things in the day of small things, and great labors if Thou summon us to any: rising and working, sitting still and suffering, according to Thy word. Go with me, and I will go; but if Thou go not with me, send me not: go before me, if Thou put me forth; let me hear Thy voice when I follow—Amen.

Christina G. Rossetti.

Almighty God, unto whom all hearts are open, all desires known, and from whom no secrets are hid; cleanse the thoughts of our hearts by the inspiration of Thy Holy Spirit, that we may perfectly love Thee, and worthily magnify Thy holy Name, through Jesus Christ our Lord—Amen.

Gregorian Sacramentary, A. D. 590.

Lord, Thy hands have formed us, and Thou hast sent us into this world, that we may walk in the way that leads to heaven and Thyself, and may find a lasting rest in Thee who art the Source and Centre of our souls. Look in pity on us poor pilgrims in the narrow way; let us not go astray, but reach at last our true home where our Father dwells. Guide and govern us from day to day, and bestow on us food and strength for body and soul, that we may journey on in peace. Forgive us for having hitherto so often wavered or looked back, and let us henceforward march straight on in the way of Thy laws, and may our last step be a safe and peaceful passage to the arms of Thy love, and the blessed fellowship of the saints in light. Hear us, O Lord, and glorify Thy name in us that we may glorify Thee for ever and ever —Amen.

Gerhard Tersteegen (1697-1769).

April the Tenth ✛ ✛ ✛ ✛ ✛ ✛ ✛ ✛ ✛

O Thou divine Spirit that, in all events of life, art knocking at the door of my heart, help me to respond to Thee. I would not be driven blindly as the stars over their courses. I would not be made to work out Thy will unwillingly, to fulfil Thy law unintelligently, to obey Thy mandates unsympathetically. I would take the events of my life as good and perfect gifts from Thee; I would receive even the sorrows of life as disguised gifts from Thee. I would have my heart open at all times to receive Thee,—at morning, noon, and night; in spring, and summer, and winter. Whether Thou comest to me in sunshine or in rain, I would take Thee into my heart joyfully. Thou art Thyself more than the sunshine, Thou art Thyself compensation for the rain; it is Thee and not Thy gifts I crave; knock, and I shall open unto Thee— Amen.

George Matheson.

April the Eleventh

Give strength, O Lord, to those who seek Thee, and continually pour into their souls the holy desire of seeking Thee; that they who long to see Thy face may not crave the world's pernicious pleasure—Amen.

Mozarabic, before A.D. 700.

Most gracious God, who governest the world with infinite wisdom and goodness, teach me contentedly to submit to the dispensations of Thy Providence, how contrary soever they may be to flesh and blood. Thou knowest the surest ways of making me happy, and art infinite in loving-kindness and mercy; therefore let Thy blessed will in everything be my choice and satisfaction. Let all my dangers awaken me to a careful performance of my duty; that I may serve Thee quietly with a devout mind, through Jesus Christ—Amen.

Robert Nelson (1656-1715).

April the Twelfth ✛ ✛ ✛ ✛ ✛ ✛ ✛ 103

O Lord, mercifully incline Thine ears to hear our prayers, and, of Thy loving-kindness, enlighten the depths of our hearts, that no evil desires may rule them—Amen.

Treasury of Devotion.

O God, who puttest into our hearts such deep desire, that we cannot be at peace until we enjoy the feeling of Thy love; mercifully grant that the unspeakable sighing of our souls' need may not go unsatisfied because of any unrighteousness of heart, which must divide us from the All-holy One; but strengthen us to do right by whomsoever we have wronged in thought, word, or deed; to renounce all plans of wrong-doing for the future; to purify our thoughts, and govern our appetites, so that we may have no bar between us and Thy glory, but enjoy Thy peace which passeth understanding—Amen.

Rowland Williams.

April the Thirteenth

O God our Father, Good beyond all that is good, Fair beyond all that is fair, in whom is calmness and peace; do Thou make up the dissensions which divide us from each other, and bring us back into an unity of love, which may bear some likeness to Thy sublime nature. Grant that we may be spiritually one, as well in ourselves as in each other, through that peace of Thine which maketh all things peaceful, and through the grace, mercy, and tenderness of Thine only Son—Amen.

Jacobite Liturgy of St. Dionysius.

Bless me, O God, with the love of Thee, and of my neighbor. Give me peace of conscience, the command of my affections; and for the rest, Thy will be done! O King of peace, keep us in love and charity—Amen.

Thomas Wilson (1663-1755).

April the Fourteenth

Lord, prepare my heart, I beseech Thee, to reverence Thee, to adore Thee, to love Thee; to hate, for love of Thee, all my sins, imperfections, shortcomings, whatever in me displeaseth Thee; and to love all which Thou lovest, and whom Thou lovest. Give me, Lord, fervor of love, shame for my unthankfulness, sorrow for my sins, longing for Thy grace, and to be wholly united with Thee. Let my very coldness call for the glow of Thy love; let my emptiness and dryness, like a barren and thirsty land, thirst for Thee, call on Thee to come into my soul, who refreshest those who are weary. Let my heart ache to Thee and for Thee, who stillest the aching of the heart. Let my mute longings praise Thee, crave to Thee, who satisfiest the empty soul, that waits on Thee—Amen.

E. B. Pusey.

April the Fifteenth

Praised be Thou, O God, Almighty Ruler, who dost make the day bright with Thy sunshine, and the night with the beams of heavenly fires! Listen now to our prayers, and forgive us both our conscious and unconscious transgressions. Clothe us with the armour of righteousness; shield us with Thy truth; watch over us with Thy power; save us from all calamity; and give us grace to pass all the days of our life, blameless, holy, peaceful, free from sin, terror, and offence. For with Thee is mercy and plenteous redemption, our Lord and God, and to Thee we bring our thanks and praise—Amen.

Greek Church.

O Lord, hear my prayer, fulfil my desire to my good, and to the praise of Thy holy name—Amen.

Sarum Breviary, A. D. 1085.

April the Sixteenth 107

Hear our prayers, O Lord, and consider our desires. Give unto us true humility, a meek and quiet spirit, a loving and a friendly, a holy and a useful manner of life; bearing the burdens of our neighbors, denying ourselves, and studying to benefit others, and to please Thee in all things. Grant us to be righteous in performing promises, loving to our relatives, careful of our charges; to be gentle and easy to be entreated, slow to anger, and readily prepared for every good work—Amen.

Jeremy Taylor (1613-1667).

O Lord, grant all who contend for the faith, never to injure it by clamor and impatience; but, speaking Thy precious truth in love, so to present it that it may be loved, and that men may see in it Thy goodness and beauty—Amen.

William Bright.

April the Seventeenth

Come, O Lord, in much mercy down into my soul, and take possession and dwell there. A homely mansion, I confess, for so glorious a Majesty, but such as Thou art fitting up for the reception of Thee, by holy and fervent desires of Thine own inspiring. Enter then, and adorn, and make it such as Thou canst inhabit, since it is the work of Thy hands. Give me Thine own self, without which, though Thou shouldst give me all that ever Thou hast made, yet could not my desires be satisfied. Let my soul ever seek Thee, and let me persist in seeking, till I have found, and am in full possession of Thee—Amen.

St. Augustine (354-430).

Most loving Lord, give me a childlike love of Thee, which may cast out all fear—Amen.

E. B. Pusey.

April the Eighteenth ✦ ✦ ✦ ✦ ✦ ✦ 109

O Lord, I give myself to Thee, I trust Thee wholly. Thou art wiser than I—more loving to me than I myself. Deign to fulfil Thy high purposes in me whatever they be—work in and through me. I am born to serve Thee, to be Thine, to be Thy instrument. Let me be Thy blind instrument. I ask not to see—I ask not to know—I ask simply to be used—Amen.

John Henry Newman.

Protect, O Lord, Thy suppliants, support their weakness, and wash away their earthly stains; and while they walk amid the darkness of this mortal life, do Thou ever quicken them by Thy light; deliver them in Thy mercy from all evils, and grant them to attain the height of good: through Jesus Christ our Lord—Amen.

Leonine Sacramentary, A. D. 440.

April the Nineteenth

Accomplish Thy perfect work in our souls, O Father; let us become day by day purer, freer, more heavenly, more happy, and preserve us unto eternal life. Bless, animate, and sustain us, and raise us mightily above all that would distract us, to Thyself and the consciousness of Thy fellowship which gives joy to all who dwell therein. As yet we are bound with many chains; we tarry among things seen and temporal, and feel their oppression; we are exposed to the storms of the outer world, and are wrestling with its ills. But we are not dismayed, for we are more than earth and dust, we are akin to Thee, O Spirit of the Lord, and can experience Thy heavenly influence. Unite us ever more closely to the company of faithful hearts whom Thou art sanctifying and preparing for heaven; fill us with their faith and love and hope—Amen.

D. A. Reinhard (1753-1812).

April the Twentieth + + + + + + 111

Lord, the Lord whose ways are right, keep us in Thy mercy from lip-service and empty forms; from having a name that we live, but being dead. Help us to worship Thee by righteous deeds and lives of holiness; that our prayer also may be set forth in Thy sight as the incense, and the lifting up of our hands be as an evening sacrifice—Amen.

Christina G. Rossetti.

Kindle in us the Fire of Thy Love; help Thou our weakness, that, strengthened in Thee and by Thee, we may take heed by good works to make our calling sure. Whatsoever our hand findeth to do, may we straightway do it, with the desire to please Thee only, and then be Thou our exceeding great Reward—Amen.

Paradise for the Christian Soul.

And now, Lord, what is my hope? Truly, my hope is even in Thee. Though I walk through the valley of the shadow of death, yet I will fear no evil. Lord, Thou knowest whereof we be made; Thou rememberest that we are but dust. I am Thine, Oh, save me! Behold, O Lord, how that I am Thy servant, and the son of Thine handmaid. Thine unprofitable servant; yet Thy servant. Thy lost prodigal child, yet Thy child. Into Thy hands I commend myself as unto a faithful Creator. Lord, I am created in Thine own image. Suffer not Thine own image to be utterly defaced, but renew it again in righteousness and true holiness. Into Thine hands I commend myself, for Thou hast redeemed me, Thou God of Truth—Amen.

Lancelot Andrewes (1555-1626).

April the Twenty-second ✢ ✢ ✢ ✢ 113

Show Thyself, O Lord, and have pity on Thy child, and bring his steps into the way of peace. Thou that knowest our thoughts, make Thyself known to our hearts; Thou, that art from everlasting, let us behold Thy truth. Hast Thou not made our souls in Thy likeness? Take away stain from the glass, and let us behold in it Thine image. When Thou willest, Thy word goeth forth; Thou breathest forth Thy love, and our souls are joined to Thee. Take away from me shame and rebuke; renew in me Thy strength, and show me the way of peace. Turn me again, and I shall be turned; take away the darkness which hideth Thee, and in the light of the living God let me see light—Amen.

Rowland Williams.

Almighty God! Eternal Treasure of all good things! Thou fillest all things with plenteousness; Thou clothest the lilies of the field, and feedest the young ravens that call upon Thee. Let Thy Providence be my store-house, my own necessities the measures of my desire; but never let my desires of this world be greedy, nor my labor immoderate, nor my care vexatious and distracting; but moderate, holy, subordinate to Thy will, the measure Thou hast appointed for me—Amen.

Jeremy Taylor (1613-1667).

Grant us, O Lord, we beseech Thee, always to seek Thy kingdom and righteousness; and of whatsoever Thou seest us to stand in need, mercifully grant us an abundant portion; through Jesus Christ our Lord—Amen.

Gelasian Sacramentary, A. D. 492.

April the Twenty-fourth ✦ ✦ ✦ ✦ 115

 **O Thou who art Love and** dwellest in love! teach us herein to be followers of Thee, as dear children. Never may we shut our hearts against the sorrows of even the unthankful and the evil. Make us organs of Thy tender mercy, to soothe the wretched, to lift the penitent, to seek and to save the lost; till all shall at length know themselves Thy children, and be one with each other and with Thee—Amen.

James Martineau.

O God, who dost bring men out of darkness and the shadow of death, such as are bound in affliction and iron, free us, we beseech Thee, from the chains of our sins, and in Thy great mercy deliver us from all evil, through Jesus Christ—Amen.

Roman Breviary.

Thou full of compassion, I commit and commend myself unto Thee, in whom I am, and live, and know. Be Thou the Goal of my pilgrimage, and my Rest by the way. Let my soul take refuge from the crowding turmoil of worldly thoughts beneath the shadow of Thy wings; let my heart, this sea of restless waves, find peace in Thee, O God. Thou bounteous Giver of all good gifts, give to him who is weary refreshing food; gather our distracted thoughts and powers into harmony again; and set the prisoner free. See, he stands at Thy door and knocks; be it opened to him, that he may enter with a free step, and be quickened by Thee. For Thou art the Well-spring of Life, the Light of eternal Brightness, wherein the just live who love Thee. Be it unto me according to Thy word— Amen.

St. Augustine (354-430).

April the Twenty-sixth ✦ ✦ ✦ ✦ ✦ 117

Almighty and most merciful God, in whom we live, and move, and have our being; Lord of all life; Source of all light, guiding and governing all things of Thy lovingkindness and power! Hear our thanksgivings unto Thee for all the joy that Thou puttest into mortal life; but chiefly for the joy that comes of sin forgiven, weakness strengthened, victory promised, life eternal looked for. To every one of us grant that, being fully conscious of having erred and strayed from Thy ways, we may be equally conscious of our need to go back again to the Good Shepherd. Let there be no doubt with any one of us that Thou dost forgive, even to the uttermost, all those who draw nigh in penitence to Thee; that so, those of us who are sinful, and sad because sinful, and sorrowful in sinning, may have this day the joy of the Lord—Amen.

George Dawson.

Merciful God, be Thou now unto me a strong tower of defence, I humbly entreat Thee. Give me grace to await Thy leisure, and patiently to bear what Thou doest unto me; nothing doubting or mistrusting Thy goodness towards me; for Thou knowest what is good for me better than I do. Therefore do with me in all things what Thou wilt; only arm me, I beseech Thee, with Thine armor, that I may stand fast; above all things, taking to me the shield of faith; praying always that I may refer myself wholly to Thy will, abiding Thy pleasure, and comforting myself in those troubles which it shall please Thee to send me, seeing such troubles are profitable for me; and I am assuredly persuaded that all Thou doest cannot but be well; and unto Thee be all honor and glory— Amen.

Lady Jane Grey, 1553.

April the Twenty-eighth ✢ ✢ ✢ ✢ 119

 **Lord, who lovest the stranger,** defend and nourish, we entreat Thee, all sojourners in strange lands and poor helpless persons, that they may glorify Thee out of grateful hearts: and to such men as are tyrannical and oppressive give searchings of spirit and amendment of ways, that Thou mayest shew mercy on them also—Amen.

Christina G. Rossetti.

God of love, who hast given a new commandment, through Thine Only-begotten Son, that we should love one another, even as Thou didst love us, the unworthy and the wandering, and gavest Thy beloved Son for our life and salvation; we pray Thee, Lord, give to us Thy servants, in all time of our life on the earth, a mind forgetful of past ill-will, a pure conscience and sincere thoughts, and a heart to love our brethren—Amen.

Coptic Liturgy of St. Cyril.

We love Thee, O our God; and we desire to love Thee more and more. Grant to us that we may love Thee as much as we desire, and as much as we ought. O dearest Friend, who hast so loved and saved us, the thought of whom is so sweet and always growing sweeter, come with Christ and dwell in our hearts; then Thou wilt keep a watch over our lips, our steps, our deeds, and we shall not need to be anxious either for our souls or our bodies. Give us love, sweetest of all gifts, which knows no enemy. Give us in our hearts pure love, born of Thy love to us, that we may love others as Thou lovest us. O most loving Father of Jesus Christ, from whom floweth all love, let our hearts, frozen in sin, cold to Thee and cold to others, be warmed by this divine fire. So help and bless us in Thy Son— Amen.

St. Anselm, tr. by James Freeman Clarke.

April the Thirtieth ✛ ✛ ✛ ✛ ✛ ✛ ✛ 121

 Almighty God, help us to put away all bitterness and wrath and evil-speaking, with all malice. May we possess our souls in patience, however we are tempted and provoked, and not be overcome with evil, but overcome evil with good. Enable us, O God of patience, to bear one another's burdens, and to forbear one another in love. Oh, teach and help us all to live in peace and to love in truth, following peace with all men and walking in love, as Christ loved us, of whom let us learn such meekness and lowliness of heart that in Him we may find rest for our souls. Subdue all bitter resentments in our minds, and let the law of kindness be in our tongues, and a meek and quiet spirit in all our lives. Make us so gentle and peaceable that we may be followers of Thee as dear children, that Thou, the God of peace, mayest dwell with us forevermore—Amen.

Benjamin Jenks (1646-1724).

O GOD, who art Thyself the exceeding great Reward of all faithful souls, grant unto us to advance daily to the utmost of our power in godliness, so that we, seeking ever that which is more perfect, may happily attain unto Thine everlasting glory—Amen.

Roman Breviary.

Almighty God, without whom we can do nothing, I firmly resolve before Thee to follow more closely the rule of Thy will; to amend my ways; to attend more diligently to the duties of my calling; to avoid all sin, and its occasions. Do Thou, who givest me the will, give me also the power to accomplish it. Grant what Thou commandest, and command what Thou wilt; that so I may live righteously in this present world, and in the world to come may praise Thee eternally—Amen.

Treasury of Devotion.

May the Second

Most merciful and gracious God, we beseech Thee to hear our prayers, and to deliver our hearts from the temptation of evil thoughts, that, by Thy goodness, we may become a fitting habitation for Thy Holy Spirit—Amen.

Priest's Prayer Book.

Almighty God, who art over all things, Life of all life,—stir in our souls, that we, being moved by Thy Spirit, may see those things which are fairest and truest in life, and clinging thereunto, be enabled to get the victory over that which is mean and base; that so at last, all evil passion and unholy desire, all self-will and contrariness to Thee, may be overcome, and we come at last to that sublime state of willing obedience, when Thy will shall be in us supreme. Of Thy mercy hear us, through Jesus Christ our Lord—Amen.

George Dawson.

Lord our God, who hast bidden the light to shine out of darkness, who hast again wakened us to praise Thy goodness and ask for Thy grace : accept now, in Thy endless mercy, the sacrifice of our worship and thanksgiving, and grant unto us all such requests as may be wholesome for us. Make us to be children of the light and of the day, and heirs of Thy everlasting inheritance. Remember, O Lord, according to the multitude of Thy mercies, Thy whole Church ; all who join with us in prayer ; all our brethren by land or sea, or wherever they may be in Thy vast kingdom, who stand in need of Thy grace and succour. Pour out upon them the riches of Thy mercy, so that we, redeemed in soul and body, and steadfast in faith, may ever praise Thy wonderful and holy name—Amen.

Greek Church.

May the Fourth ✦ ✦ ✦ ✦ ✦ ✦ ✦ ✦ 125

Lord, because being compassed with infirmities we oftentimes sin and ask pardon, help us to forgive as we would be forgiven; neither mentioning old offences committed against us, nor dwelling upon them in thought, nor being influenced by them in heart: but loving our brother freely as Thou freely lovest us—Amen.

Christina G. Rossetti.

Blessed Lord, I beseech Thee to pour down upon me such grace as may not only cleanse this life of mine, but beautify it a little, if it be Thy will,—before I go hence and am no more seen. Grant that I may love Thee with all my heart and soul and mind and strength, and my neighbor as myself—and that I may persevere unto the end; through Jesus Christ—Amen.

James Skinner (1818–1882).

Nothing, O Lord, is liker to Thy holy nature than the mind that is settled in quietness. Thou hast called us into that quietness and peace of Thine, from out of the turmoils of this world, as it were, from out of storms into a haven; which is such a peace as the world cannot give, and as passeth all capacity of man. Grant now, O most merciful Father, that, through Thine exceeding goodness, our minds may yield themselves obedient unto Thee without striving; and that they may quietly rise into that sovereign rest of Thine above. Grant that nothing may disturb or disquiet them here beneath; but that all things may be quiet and calm through that peace of Thine—Amen.

A Book of Christian Prayers, A.D. 1578.

May the Sixth

Gracious Father, keep me through Thy Holy Spirit; keep my heart soft and tender now in health and amidst the bustle of the world; keep the thought of Thyself present to me as my Father in Jesus Christ; and keep alive in me a spirit of love and meekness to all men, that I may be at once gentle and active and firm. O strengthen me to bear pain, or sickness, or danger, or whatever Thou shalt be pleased to lay upon me, as Christ's soldier and servant; and let my faith overcome the world daily. Perfect and bless the work of Thy Spirit in the hearts of all Thy people, and may Thy kingdom come, and Thy will be done in earth as it is in heaven. I pray for this, and for all that Thou seest me to need, for Jesus Christ's sake—Amen.

Thomas Arnold.

May the Seventh

 Lord, help us by prayer to hold Thee fast, and by love to cleave steadfastly unto Thee, our ever-present Aid. We entreat Thee, when Thy Providences are dark to our eyes strengthen our faith; and whatever portion Thou allottest to us, give us grace to say, It is enough—Amen.

Christina G. Rossetti.

 God, whose mercy reacheth unto the heavens, and Thy righteousness unto the clouds, teach me to abhor everything which is evil, and to set myself in every good way; that, my trust being under the shadow of Thy wings, I may rejoice in Thy loving-kindness all the days of my life; and at last may be satisfied with the plenteousness of Thy house, and in the light of Thy countenance may see everlasting light, through Jesus Christ our Lord—Amen.

Jeremy Taylor, 1613-1667.

Almighty God, by whose word all things work, by whose guidance all things go, so order our inward life, that we may be enabled to understand the things that we see; and by Thy guidance in the spiritual life and in charity, so order what there is disordered in our lives, so bring our minds to the truth, our consciences to the law, our eyes to the light, and our hearts to Thy true love, that, amidst the seeming discords of life, we may hear the music of the heavenly will, and catch ofttimes the charms of the heavenly order. So give us hope that we may pass on through time, into the higher and better education of the eternal life to come, and that at last we may know those things that are hidden, and which now we cannot know, and learn the glorious beauty and the glorious loving of the eternal years—Amen.

George Dawson.

**I** **Offer up unto Thee my prayers** and intercessions, for those especially who have in any matter hurt, grieved, or found fault with me, or who have done me any damage or displeasure.

For all those also whom, at any time, I may have vexed, troubled, burdened, and scandalized, by words or deeds, knowingly or in ignorance; that Thou wouldst grant us all equally pardon for our sins, and for our offences against each other.

Take away from our hearts, O Lord, all suspiciousness, indignation, wrath, and contention, and whatsoever may hurt charity, and lessen brotherly love.

Have mercy, O Lord, have mercy on those that crave Thy mercy, give grace unto them that stand in need thereof, and make us such as that we may be worthy to enjoy Thy grace, and go forward to life eternal—Amen.

Thomas à Kempis.

May the Tenth ✣ ✣ ✣ ✣ ✣ ✣ ✣ ✣ ✣ 131

The fetters Thou imposest, O Lord, are wings of freedom. There is no liberty like the liberty of being bound to go. When Thou layest upon me the sense of obligation, that moment Thou settest my spirit free. When Thou sayest that I must, my heart says, "I can." My strength is proportionate to the strength of those cords that bind me. I am never so unrestrained as when I am constrained by Thy love. Evermore, Thou Divine Spirit, guide me by this instinct of the right. Put round about my heart the cord of Thy captivating love, and draw me whither in my own light I would not go. Bind me to Thyself as Thou bindest the planets to the sun, that it may become the very law of my nature to be led by Thee. May I be content to know that goodness and mercy shall *follow* me without waiting to see them in advance of me—Amen.

George Matheson.

May the Eleventh

We ask not, O Father, for health or life. We make an offering to Thee of all our days. Thou hast counted them. We would know nothing more. All we ask is to die rather than live unfaithful to Thee; and, if it be Thy will that we depart, let us die in patience and love. Almighty God, who holdest in Thy hand the keys of the grave to open and close it at Thy will, give us not life, if we shall love it too well. Living or dying we would be Thine—Amen.

François de la Mothe Fénelon (1651–1715).

O God, Author of eternal light, do Thou shed forth continual day upon us who watch for Thee; that our lips may praise Thee, our life may bless Thee, our meditations may glorify Thee; through Christ our Lord—Amen.

Sarum Breviary, A. D. 1085.

May the Twelfth ✢ ✢ ✢ ✢ ✢ ✢ ✢ 133

**O Lord, with whom are Strength** and Wisdom, put forth Thy strength, I implore Thee, for Thine own sake and for our sakes, and stand up to help us; for we are deceivable and weak persons, frail and brief, unstable and afraid, unless Thou put the might of Thy Holy Spirit within us—Amen, O Lord—Amen.

Christina G. Rossetti.

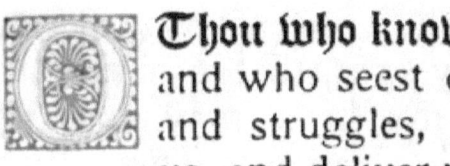**O Thou who knowest our hearts,** and who seest our temptations and struggles, have pity upon us, and deliver us from the sins which make war upon our souls. Thou art all-powerful, and we are weak and erring. Our trust is in Thee, O Thou faithful and good God. Deliver us from the bondage of evil, and grant that we may hereafter be Thy devoted servants, serving Thee in the freedom of holy love, for Christ's sake—Amen.

Eugène Bersier.

May the Thirteenth

Ah, Lord unto whom all hearts are open, Thou canst govern the vessel of my soul far better than I can. Arise, O Lord, and command the stormy wind and the troubled sea of my heart to be still, and at peace in Thee, that I may look up to Thee undisturbed, and abide in union with Thee, my Lord. Let me not be carried hither and thither by wandering thoughts; but, forgetting all else, let me see and hear Thee. Renew my spirit; kindle in me Thy light, that it may shine within me, and my heart may burn in love and adoration towards Thee. Let Thy Holy Spirit dwell in me continually, and make me Thy temple and sanctuary, and fill me with divine love and light and life, with devout and heavenly thoughts, with comfort and strength, with joy and peace—Amen.

Johann Arndt (1555-1621).

May the Fourteenth ✦ ✦ ✦ ✦ ✦ ✦ 135

God, who hast commanded us to be perfect, as Thou our Father in heaven art perfect: put into our hearts, we pray Thee, a continual desire to obey Thy holy will. Teach us day by day what Thou wouldest have us do, and give us grace and power to fulfil the same. May we never from love of ease, decline the path which Thou pointest out, nor, for fear of shame, turn away from it—Amen.

Henry Alford.

Grant, O Lord, that my petitions may always be for those things that may fit me to please Thee, and not for such as may be the fittest to please myself; and, for an accumulation of blessings, so influence my soul with Thy divine Spirit, that Thy will may ever be my pleasure—Amen.

Charles How (1661–1745).

May the Fifteenth

God, who art Peace everlasting, whose chosen reward is the gift of peace, and who hast taught us that the peacemakers are Thy children, pour Thy peace into our souls, that everything discordant may utterly vanish, and all that makes for peace be sweet to us forever—Amen.

Mozarabic, before A. D. 700.

Lord, who art a God ready to pardon, and of great kindness, remove far from me all occasions and effects of causeless and inordinate anger. Give me a mild, a peaceable, a meek, and an humble spirit, that, remembering my own infirmities, I may bear with those of others; that I may think lowly of myself, and not be angry when others also think lowly of me; that I may be patient towards all men, gentle and easy to be entreated; that God may be so towards me—Amen.

Thomas Wilson (1663-1755).

May the Sixteenth ✦ ✦ ✦ ✦ ✦ ✦ ✦ 137

We pray Thee to compassionate our weakness, O Lord, to guard us in peril, to direct us in doubt, and to save us from falling into sin. From the evil that is around and within us, graciously deliver us. Make the path of duty plain before us, and keep us in it even unto the end—Amen.

King's Chapel Liturgy (1831).

We humbly beseech Thee, O heavenly Father, to do away as the night all our transgressions, and to scatter our sins as the morning cloud. Lord, forgive whatsoever is amiss in us, cleanse us from our sin, and let Thy Holy Spirit so prevent and accompany and follow us day by day, that we may believe in Thee, and love Thee, and keep Thy commandments, through Jesus Christ our Lord—Amen.

Goulburn's Family Prayers.

May the Seventeenth

Late have I loved Thee, O Thou Eternal Truth and Goodness: late have I sought Thee, my Father! But Thou didst seek me, and when Thou shinedst forth upon me, then I knew Thee and learnt to love Thee. I thank Thee, O my Light, that Thou didst thus shine upon me; that Thou didst teach my soul what Thou wouldst be to me, and didst incline Thy face in pity unto me. Thou, Lord, hast become my Hope, my Comfort, my Strength, my All! In Thee doth my soul rejoice. The darkness vanished from before mine eyes, and I beheld Thee, the Sun of Righteousness. When I loved darkness, I knew Thee not, but wandered on from night to night. But Thou didst lead me out of that blindness; Thou didst take me by the hand and call me to Thee, and now I can thank Thee, and Thy mighty voice which hath penetrated to my inmost heart—Amen.

St. Augustine (354-430).

God, our Everliving Refuge! With grateful hearts we lay at Thy feet the folded hours when Thou knowest us but we know not Thee; and with joy receive from Thy hand once more our open task and conscious communion with Thy life and thought. Day by day liken us more to the spirits of the departed wise and good; and fit us in our generation to carry on their work below till we are ready for more perfect union with them above. And if ever we faint under any appointed cross and say, "It is too hard to bear," may we look to the steps of the Man of Sorrows toiling on to Calvary, and pass freely into Thy hand, and become one with Him and Thee. Dedicate us to the joyful service of Thy will; and own us as Thy children in time and in eternity—Amen.

James Martineau.

May the Nineteenth

Almighty God, Father of mercies, be pleased to work in me what Thou hast commanded should be in me. Give me, O Lord, the grace of an earnest sorrow,—turn my sin into repentance, and let my repentance proceed to pardon; and teach me so diligently to watch over all my actions that I may never transgress Thy holy laws willingly, but that it may be the work of my life to obey Thee, the joy of my soul to please Thee, and the perfection of my desires to live with Thee in the kingdom of Thy grace and glory—Amen.

Jeremy Taylor (1613-1667).

O God, the Life of the faithful, the Bliss of the righteous : mercifully receive the prayers of thy suppliants, that the souls which thirst for thy promises may evermore be filled from thine abundance, through Jesus Christ our Lord—Amen.

Gelasian, A. D. 492.

May the Twentieth

O God, my God, give me a heart to thank Thee; lift up my heart above myself, to Thee and Thine eternal throne; let it not linger here among the toils and turmoils of this lower world; let it not be oppressed by any earth-born clouds of care or anxiety or fear or suspicion; but bind it wholly to Thee and to Thy love; give me eyes to see Thy love in all things, and Thy grace in all around me; make me to thank Thee for Thy love and Thy grace to all and in all; give me wings of love, that I may soar up to Thee, and cling to Thee, and adore Thee, and praise Thee more and more, until I be fitted to enter into the joys of Thine everlasting love, everlastingly to love Thee and Thy grace, whereby Thou didst make me such as Thou couldest love, such as could love Thee, O God, my God—Amen.

E. B. Pusey.

May the Twenty-first

Faithful Lord, grant to us, I pray Thee, faithful hearts devoted to Thee, and to the service of all men for Thy sake. Fill us with pure love of Thee, keep us steadfast in this love, give us faith that worketh by love, and preserve us faithful unto death—Amen.

Christina G. Rossetti.

Almighty and merciful God, who dost grant unto Thy faithful people the grace to make every path of life temporal the straight and narrow way which leadeth unto life eternal, grant that we, who know that we have no strength as of ourselves to help ourselves, and therefore do put all our trust in Thine Almighty power, may, by the assistance of Thy heavenly grace, always prevail in all things, against whatsoever shall arise to fight against us; through Jesus Christ—Amen.

Roman Breviary.

May the Twenty-second ✦ ✦ ✦ ✦ 143

Shepherd of the sheep, who didst promise to carry the lambs in Thine arms, and to lead us by the still waters, help us to know the peace which passeth understanding. Give us to drink that heavenly draught which is life, the calm patience which is content to bear what God giveth. Have mercy upon us, and hear our prayers. Lead us gently when we pass through the valley of the shadow of death. Guide us, till at last, in the assembly of Thy saints, we may find rest forevermore—Amen.
George Dawson.

God, of surpassing goodness, whom the round world with one voice doth praise for Thy sweet benignity; we pray Thee to remove from us all error, that so we may perform Thy will; through Jesus Christ our Lord—Amen.
Sarum Breviary, A. D. 1085.

L

May the Twenty-third

Holy Spirit, who, in all ages hast comforted and strengthened martyrs and confessors; who hast ever been the sustaining comfort and sweet refreshment of the sorrowful and the suffering; who sheddest abroad love, joy, and peace, in the hearts of the faithful and obedient followers of Christ; grant that we may be filled with all the fulness of Thy gifts of grace; that, by Thy holy inspiration, we may think those things that be good, and, by Thy merciful guiding, may perform the same—Amen.
Treasury of Devotion, 1869.

Heavenly King, Thou Comforter and Spirit of truth, who art in every place, and fillest the whole world with the treasures of Thy goodness; O Life-giver, come into our hearts and dwell there, and save our souls alive, and unto Thee be glory now and evermore—Amen.
Book of Hours, 1865.

May the Twenty-fourth + + + + + 145

O God, **who makest cheerfulness** the companion of strength, but apt to take wings in time of sorrow, we humbly beseech Thee that if, in Thy sovereign wisdom, Thou sendest weakness, yet for Thy mercy's sake deny us not the comfort of patience. Lay not more upon us, O heavenly Father, than Thou wilt enable us to bear; and, since the fretfulness of our spirits is more hurtful than the heaviness of our burden, grant us that heavenly calmness which comes of owning Thy hand in all things, and patience in the trust that Thou doest all things well—Amen.

Rowland Williams.

Grant, **we beseech Thee, Almighty** God, that we, who in our tribulation are yet of good cheer because of Thy lovingkindness, may find Thee mighty to save from all dangers, through Jesus Christ—Amen.

Roman Breviary.

May the Twenty-fifth

 King of Glory, bring us all home, I pray Thee, by grace unto glory. Let our light affliction which is but for a moment work for us a far more exceeding and eternal weight of glory—Amen.

Christina G. Rossetti.

 God, who hast ordained that whatever is to be desired, should be sought by labor, and who, by Thy blessing, bringest honest labor to good effect; look with mercy upon my studies and endeavors. Grant me, O Lord, to design only what is lawful and right; and afford me calmness of mind, and steadiness of purpose, that I may so do Thy will in this short life, as to obtain happiness in the world to come, for the sake of Jesus Christ our Lord—Amen.

Samuel Johnson (1709-1784).

May the Twenty-sixth ✦ ✦ ✦ ✦ ✦ 147

Lord, our God, great, eternal, wonderful in glory, who keepest covenant and promises for those that love Thee with their whole heart; who art the Life of all, the Help of those that flee unto Thee, the Hope of those who cry unto Thee; cleanse us from our sins, secret and open, and from every thought displeasing to Thy goodness,—cleanse our bodies and souls, our hearts and consciences, that with a pure heart and a clear soul, with perfect love and calm hope, we may venture confidently and fearlessly to pray unto Thee—Amen.

Coptic Liturgy of St. Basil.

Lord, keep me ever near to Thee. Let nothing separate me from Thee, let nothing keep me back from Thee. If I fall, bring me back quickly to Thee, and make me hope in Thee, trust in Thee, love Thee everlastingly—Amen.

E. B. Pusey.

Great and lofty God, Thou Father in the Highest, who hast promised to dwell with them that are of a lowly spirit and fear Thy word; create now in us such lowly hearts, and give us a reverential awe of Thy commandments. O come, Thou Holy Spirit, and kindle our hearts with holy love; come, Thou Spirit of Strength, and arouse our souls to hunger and thirst after Thee, their true Guide, that they may be sustained by Thy all-powerful influence. Arise, O Spirit of Life, that through Thee we may begin to live; descend upon us and transform us into such human beings as the heart of God longs to see us, renewed into the image of Christ, and going on from glory to glory. O God, Thou Supreme Good, make Thyself known to us, and glorify Thyself in our inner being—Amen.

Gerhard Tersteegen, 1731.

May the Twenty-eighth ✦ ✦ ✦ ✦ ✦ 149

 **Make Thy way plain before** my face. Support me this day under all the difficulties I shall meet with. I offer myself to Thee, O God, this day to do in me, and with me, as to Thee seems most meet—Amen.

Thomas Wilson (1663-1755).

Almighty God, who wast, and art, and art to come, Eternal Home of man, Refuge of the weary, Strength of the weak,—of Thy loving-kindness and tender mercy grant unto us that we, being guided by Thy good Spirit, and coming with lowly hearts unto Thee, may know Thy truth, feel Thy light, drink of the living water, and eat of the bread of heaven; and that, passing through the gate of death, we may enter at last into the life everlasting, through Jesus Christ our Lord—Amen.

George Dawson.

May the Twenty-ninth

Our Father, unto Thee, in the light of our Saviour's blessed Life, we would lift our souls. We thank Thee for that true Light shining in our world with still increasing brightness. We thank Thee for all who have walked therein, and especially for those near to us and dear, in whose lives we have seen this excellent glory and beauty. May we know that in the body and out of the body they are with Thee, and that when these earthly days come to an end, it is not that our service of Thee and of one another may cease, but that it may begin anew. Make us glad in all who have faithfully lived ; make us glad in all who have peacefully died. Lift us into light and love and purity and blessedness, and give us at last our portion with those who have trusted in Thee and sought, in small things as in great, in things temporal and things eternal, to do Thy Holy Will —Amen.

Rufus Ellis.

May the Thirtieth ✤ ✤ ✤ ✤ ✤ ✤ ✤ 151

 Lord, grant us grace never to parley with temptation, never to tamper with conscience; never to spare the right eye, or hand, or foot that is a snare to us; never to lose our souls, though in exchange we should gain the whole world—Amen.

Christina G. Rossetti.

Heavenly Father, the Father of all wisdom, understanding, and true strength, I beseech Thee, look mercifully upon me, and send Thy Holy Spirit into my breast; that when I must join to fight in the field for the glory of Thy holy Name, then I, being strengthened with the defence of Thy right hand, may manfully stand in the confession of Thy faith, and of Thy truth, and continue in the same unto the end of my life, through our Lord Jesus Christ—Amen.

Nicholas Ridley (1500–1555).

May the Thirty-first

We give Thee thanks, yea, more than thanks, O Lord our God, for all Thy goodness at all times and in all places, because Thou hast shielded, rescued, helped, and guided us all the days of our lives, and brought us unto this hour. We pray and beseech Thee, merciful God, to grant in Thy goodness that we may spend this day, and all the time of our lives, without sin, in fulness of joy, holiness, and reverence of Thee. But drive away from us, O Lord, all envy, all fear, and all temptations. Bestow upon us what is good and meet. Whatever sin we commit in thought, word, or deed, do Thou in Thy goodness and mercy be pleased to pardon. And lead us not into temptation, but deliver us from evil, through the grace, mercy, and love of Thine only begotten Son—Amen.

Liturgy of St. Mark (175-254?).

June the First — 153

I humbly adore Thy glorious Majesty, for having given me a capacity of loving, obeying, and contemplating Thee; and, consequently, a foretaste of happiness eternal, in the adoration of Thee. Give me, I implore Thee, a power to exercise this privilege in the most perfect manner that Thy infinite bounty shall enable me to do; and grant that the remainder of my life may be spent in the exactest performance of every part of my duty to Thee; for Jesus Christ's sake—Amen.

Charles How (1661-1745).

Be our Shepherd, O Lord, we entreat Thee, and may we receive all good things from Thy sweetness; so that, obtaining an eternal habitation in Thy tabernacles, we may be filled with the plenteousness of Thine everlasting cup, through Christ our Lord—Amen.

Sarum Breviary, A. D. 1085.

Most merciful God and Father, we commend ourselves and all that we have to Thine Almighty hands, and pray Thee to preserve us by Thy good Spirit from all sin, misfortune, and grief of heart. Give us the Spirit of grace and prayer, that we may have a consoling trust in Thy love, and that our sighs and petitions may be acceptable in Thy sight. Give us the Spirit of faith to kindle a bright flame of true and blessed faith in our hearts, that we may have a living knowledge of salvation, and our whole life may be a thank-offering for the mercies we have received. Give us the Spirit of love, that we may experience the sweetness of Thy love toward us, and also love Thee in return; and render our obedience not from constraint like slaves, but with the willing and joyful hearts of children—Amen.

Gottfried Arnold, 1697.

June the Third · · · · · · · · · 155

Grant, Lord, that I may not, for one moment, admit willingly into my soul any thought contrary to Thy love—Amen.

E. B. Pusey.

Almighty God, grant that by the faithful practice of the things that we know to be true, our hearts may be purged of all evil thoughts and desires, and we be brought back again to something of the pureness of spirit by which alone Thou mayest be served. Forgive all our wanderings from the light. Grant that we may escape this great condemnation—that light having come into the world, we have chosen darkness rather than light. Show us the light, and cause us to live in it, and by it to pass through the shadow of death with safety, and to abide with it for evermore. Hear us of Thy mercy, through Jesus Christ our Lord—Amen.

George Dawson.

O Lord my God, for life and reason, nurture, preservation, guidance, education; for Thy gifts of grace and nature, for Thy calling, recalling, manifold recalling me again and again. For Thy forbearance, long-suffering, and long long-suffering toward me, even until now; for all from whom I have received any good or help; for the use of Thy present good things; for Thy promise, and my hope, of good things to come.

For all these things, and for all other, which I know, which i know not, manifest or secret, remembered or forgotten by me, I praise Thee, I bless Thee, I give Thee thanks; and I will praise, and bless, and give Thee thanks, all the days of my life.

What shall I render unto the Lord for all His benefits to me? Thou art worthy, O Lord, to receive glory, and honor, and power—Amen.

Lancelot Andrewes (1555-1626).

June the Fifth ✚ ✚ ✚ ✚ ✚ ✚ ✚ ✚ 157

Lord, who knowest all things, and lovest all men better than Thou knowest, Thine is might and wisdom and love to save us.

As our fathers called unto Thee, and were holpen, and were led along the ways Thou seest good ; so, in all time of need, from all evil, the evil of our time and of our hearts, deliver us, good Lord.

From all perplexity of mind ; from loneliness of thought, and discontented brooding; from wondering what Thou wouldst have us do, deliver us, Lord. Especially from whatever sin besets us, save and deliver us with might, O Lord.

From all bereavement, sorrow, and desertion; from all things that separate us from each other and from our God ; from all evils we have prayed against, and from all we have not thought of, deliver, O Lord, Thy servants, whose hope is in Thy goodness for ever—Amen.

Rowland Williams.

In Thee, O Lord God, I place my whole hope and refuge; on Thee I rest all my tribulation and anguish; for I find all to be weak and inconstant, whatsoever I behold out of Thee. For many friends cannot profit, nor strong helpers assist, nor the books of the learned afford comfort, nor any place, however retired and lovely, give shelter, unless Thou Thyself dost assist, strengthen, console, instruct, and guard us. For all things that seem to belong to the attainment of peace and felicity, without Thee, are nothing, and do bring in truth no felicity at all. Thou therefore art the Fountain of all that is good; and to hope in Thee above all things, is the strongest comfort of Thy servants. To Thee, therefore, do I lift up mine eyes; in Thee, my God, the Father of mercies, do I put my trust—Amen.

Thomas à Kempis.

June the Seventh ✦ ✦ ✦ ✦ ✦ ✦ ✦ 159

O Lord, give us more charity, more self-denial, more likeness to Thee. Teach us to sacrifice our comforts to others, and our likings for the sake of doing good. Make us kindly in thought, gentle in word, generous in deed. Teach us that it is better to give than to receive; better to forget ourselves than to put ourselves forward; better to minister than to be ministered unto. And unto Thee, the God of Love, be glory and praise for ever—Amen.

Henry Alford.

O Lord, move us by Thine example to show kindness and do good. Grant us such patience and forbearance with all sufferers gracious or ungracious, grateful or ungrateful; that in our stumbling walk and scant measure they may yet discern a vestige of Thee, and give Thee the glory—Amen.

Christina G. Rossetti.

June the Eighth

O God, the Light of every heart that sees Thee, the Life of every soul that loves Thee, the Strength of every mind that seeks Thee, grant me ever to continue steadfast in Thy holy love. Be Thou the joy of my heart; take it all to Thyself, and therein abide. The house of my soul is, I confess, too narrow for Thee; do Thou enlarge it, that Thou mayest enter in; it is ruinous, but do Thou repair it. It has that within which must offend Thine eyes; I confess and know it; but whose help shall I implore in cleansing it, but Thine alone? To Thee, therefore, I cry urgently, begging that Thou wilt cleanse me from my secret faults, and keep Thy servant from presumptuous sins, that they never get dominion over me—Amen.

St. Augustine (354–430).

O Lord, forgive what I have been, sanctify what I am; and order what I shall be—Amen.

June the Ninth ✦ ✦ ✦ ✦ ✦ ✦ ✦ ✦ 161

Incline, O Lord, Thy merciful ears, and illuminate the darkness of our hearts by the light of Thy visitation—Amen.
Gelasian Sacrametary, A. D. 492.

Almighty God, Lord of the storm and of the calm, the vexed sea and the quiet haven, of day and of night, of life and of death,—grant unto us so to have our hearts stayed upon Thy faithfulness, Thine unchangingness and love, that, whatsoever betide us, however black the cloud or dark the night, with quiet faith trusting in Thee, we may look upon Thee with untroubled eye, and walking in lowliness towards Thee, and in lovingness towards one another, abide all storms and troubles of this mortal life, beseeching Thee that they may turn to the soul's true good. We ask it for Thy mercy's sake, shown in Jesus Christ our Lord—Amen.
George Dawson.

O Thou God of Peace, unite our hearts by Thy bond of peace, that we may live with one another continually in gentleness and humility, in peace and unity. O Thou God of Patience, give us patience in the time of trial, and steadfastness to endure to the end. O Thou Spirit of prayer, awaken our hearts, that we may lift up holy hands to God, and cry unto Him in all our distresses. O Thou gentle Wind, cool and refresh our hearts in all heat and anguish. Be our Defence and Shade in the time of need, our Help in trial, our Consolation when all things are against us. Come, O Thou eternal Light, Salvation, and Comfort, be our Light in darkness, our Salvation in life, our Comfort in death; and lead us in the straight way to everlasting life, that we may praise Thee, forever—Amen.

Bernhard Albrecht (1569–1636).

June the Eleventh ✢ ✢ ✢ ✢ ✢ ✢ ✢ 163

I Bless Thee, my Father and my Friend, for all that Thou hast given me, and for all that Thou hast taken from me; for all my trials and sorrows, as well as for all my joys. Thou hast mercifully led me through this wilderness, and hast borne with my many shortcomings and evil-doings. Thou art indeed most gracious and glorious, a Father of mercies, and a God of love. Rouse this sluggish heart of mine, and fill it with gratitude. And be with me, Lord, for the time to come. I know not what is before me, but Thou knowest. Choose Thou my portion for me. Lead me by Thine own hand; and keep me close to Thee, day by day, and night by night. My Father, I wish to love and obey Thee. Take my heart, for I cannot give it to Thee; and put away everything that hinders me from being altogether Thine—Amen.

Ashton Oxenden.

June the Twelfth

Lord, Faithful Creator, give us grace, we entreat Thee, in well doing and with full assurance of faith, to commit the keeping of our souls to Thee, and rest in Thy promises. And help us that we may always speak the truth; and though it be to our own hindrance, keep faith one with another—Amen.

Christina G. Rossetti.

O God, grant that for the time to come, I may yield a cheerful obedience to all Thy appointments. Remember me in the day of trouble; keep me from all excess of fear, concern, and sadness. Grant me an humble and resigned heart, that, with perfect control I may ever acquiesce in all the methods of Thy grace; that I may never frustrate the designs of Thy mercy by unreasonable fears, by sloth, or self-love—Amen.

Thomas Wilson (1663-1755).

June the Thirteenth ✦ ✦ ✦ ✦ ✦ ✦ 165

I Worship Thee, O my God, with all my best love and awe, with my fervent affection, with my most subdued, most resolved will. O make my heart beat with Thy heart. Purify it of all that is earthly, all that is proud and sensual, all that is hard and cruel, of all perversity, of all disorder, of all deadness. So fill it with Thee, that neither the events of the day nor the circumstances of the time may have power to ruffle it ; but that in Thy love and Thy fear it may have peace—Amen.

John Henry Newman.

O God, who in Thy loving-kindness dost both begin and finish all good things; grant that as we glory in the beginnings of Thy grace, so we may rejoice in its completion ; through Jesus Christ our Lord—Amen.

Leonine Sacramentary, A. D. 440.

June the Fourteenth

Thou most sweet and loving Lord, Thou knowest mine infirmities, and the necessities which I endure; in how great evils and sins I am involved; how often I am weighed down, tempted, and disturbed by them. I entreat of Thee consolation and support. I speak to Thee who knowest all things, to whom all my inward thoughts are open, and who alone canst perfectly comfort and help me. Thou knowest what things I stand in most need of. Behold, I stand before Thee poor and naked, calling for grace, and imploring mercy. Refresh Thy hungry supplicant, kindle my coldness with the fire of Thy love, enlighten my blindness with the brightness of Thy presence. Suffer me not to go away from Thee hungry and dry, but deal mercifully with me, as oftentimes Thou hast dealt wonderfully with Thy saints— Amen.

Thomas a Kempis.

June the Fifteenth

Grant unto us, Almighty God, in all time of sore distress, the comfort of the forgiveness of our sins. In time of darkness give us blessed hope, in time of sickness of body give us quiet courage; and when the heart is bowed down, and the soul is very heavy, and life is a burden, and pleasure a weariness, and the sun is too bright, and life too mirthful, then may that Spirit, the Spirit of the Comforter, come upon us, and after our darkness may there be the clear shining of the heavenly light; that so, being uplifted again by Thy mercy, we may pass on through this our mortal life with quiet courage, patient hope, and unshaken trust, hoping through Thy loving-kindness and tender mercy to be delivered from death into the large life of the eternal years. Hear us of Thy mercy, through Jesus Christ our Lord—Amen.

George Dawson.

O Lord, God of our fathers, we bless Thy holy name, Thy grace and mercy, for all those who have gone before us to rest in Thee; all, in all vocations, who have pleased Thee. And, we pray Thee, give us also grace to walk before Thee as they walked in righteousness and self-denial, that, having labored as they labored, we may afterwards rest as they rest—Amen.

Christina G. Rossetti.

✠

Almighty and Holy Spirit, the Comforter, pure, living, true,—illuminate, govern, sanctify me, and confirm my heart and mind in the faith, and in all genuine consolation; preserve and rule over me that, dwelling in the house of the Lord all the days of my life, to behold the beauty of the Lord, I may be and remain forever in the temple of the Lord, and praise Him with a joyful spirit, and in union with all the heavenly church—Amen.

Philip Melancthon (1497-1560).
(From his last prayer.)

June the Seventeenth ✦ ✦ ✦ ✦ ✦ 169

Give, I pray Thee, to all children grace reverently to love their parents, and lovingly to obey them. Teach us all that filial duty never ends or lessens: and bless all parents in their children, and all children in their parents. O Thou in whom the fatherless find mercy, make all orphans, I beseech Thee, loving and dutiful unto Thee, their true Father. Be Thy will their law, Thy house their home, Thy love their inheritance. And I earnestly pray Thee, comfort those who have lost their children, giving mothers grace to be comforted though they are not; and grant us all faith to yield our dearest treasures unto Thee with joy and thanksgiving, that where with Thee our treasure is, there our hearts may be also. Thus may we look for and hasten unto the day of union with Thee, and of reunion—Amen.

Christina G. Rossetti.

June the Eighteenth

Lord, do not permit my trials to be above my strength; and do Thou vouchsafe to be my strength and comfort in the time of trial. Give me grace to take in good part whatever shall befall me; and let my heart acknowledge it to be the Lord's doing, and to come from Thy Providence, and not by chance. May I receive everything from Thy hand with patience and with joy—Amen.

Thomas Wilson (1663-1755).

Lord, who orderest all things for us in infinite wisdom and love, who knowest my weakness, and every beating and aching of my heart, blindly I, blind, give myself unto Thy tender loving heart. Only give me grace to think, speak, act, feel, as shall please Thy love—Amen.

E. B. Pusey.

June the Nineteenth ✦ ✦ ✦ ✦ ✦ 171

 Lord, long-suffering and abundant in Goodness and Truth, fill us, I beseech Thee, with graces. Make us long-suffering and patient, cordial and sympathizing, kind and good; teach us to hold and speak the truth in love, and to shew mercy that we also obtain mercy—Amen.

Christina G. Rossetti.

Lord God Almighty, who art our true Peace, and Love eternal; enlighten our souls with the brightness of Thy peace, and purify our consciences with the sweetness of Thy love, that we may with peaceful hearts wait for the Author of peace, and in the adversities of this world may ever have Thee for our Guardian and Protector; and so being fenced about by Thy care, may heartily give ourselves to the love of Thy peace—Amen.

Mozarabic, before A.D. 700.

June the Twentieth

My Refuge and my Lord, I believe and hope in Thee, and with my whole heart I love Thee. Behold Thou hast set before me death and life, sorrows and joys, hopes and fears; towards what shall I stretch forth my hand? O Lord, I know not, but Thou knowest; do with me what pleaseth Thee. Thine am I with my whole heart. My times are in Thy hand. O Thou, my only Hope, Thy will be done as in heaven so on earth. Be that done, be that done,—not what I will, but what Thou wilt. Henceforth, even for ever, I cast all my care upon Thee, for I know that Thou carest for me, yea, even for me; hide me under the shadow of Thy wings. Let Thy will be done! I will wait in silence for Thy salvation, O my God, and I will love Thee with my whole heart—Amen.

The Way of Eternal Life.

June the Twenty-first ✤ ✤ ✤ ✤ 173

O Lord God Almighty, redeem my soul from its bondage, that I may be free to live henceforth, not for myself but for Thee. Help me to put away self, and to remember that this life is not given for my ease, my enjoyment. It is a schooling time for the eternal home Thou hast prepared for those who love Thee. Keep my eye steadily fixed on that haven of rest and peace, that I may not faint nor be weary from the length of the way, but may strive to walk worthy of my high calling in all meekness and lowliness of heart. And after that I have suffered awhile, when I am strengthened, stablished, settled in Thy love, when I have done all the work Thou hast for me to do, O gracious God, be with me to guide me through the valley of the shadow of death, and, in Thine own good time, take me to dwell with Thee—Amen.

Maria Hare.

Father, with thankful and humble hearts we appear before Thee. We would thank Thee for all the benefits that we have received from Thy goodness : It is to Thy blessing we owe what success we have found. Every opportunity for doing good ; every impulse in the right way ; each victory we have gained over ourselves ; every thought of Thy presence, O Father ; every silent but loving glance on the example of our Pattern, Thy Son our Lord—all are alike Thy gifts to us. Give us strength and wisdom to walk faithfully and joyfully in the way of willing obedience to Thy laws, and cheerful trust in Thy love. The best thanksgiving we can offer to Thee is to live according to Thy holy will ; grant us every day to offer it more perfectly, and to grow in the knowledge of Thy will and the love thereof, for evermore—Amen.

Michael Sailer (1751-1832).

June the Twenty-third

I Ask, dear Lord, that Thou wouldest make me wholly Thine. Penetrate me wholly with Thyself, that Thou mayest be all in all in me; be Thou the Soul of my soul. Lord, I am weary of myself, weary of being so unlike Thee, of being so far away from Thee. Abide with me, then,—abide in me. Let no sorrow keep me away from Thee; let no loneliness or desolation of soul affright me. Let me not think of Thee as one afar off; let me not think of Thee as a severe judge, since Thou Thyself comest unto me, and fallest on the neck of Thy poor prodigal, and givest me the kiss of peace. Thou wilt not let those go empty away who come to Thee from far. Lord, I am come to Thee from far, the far-off land of my miseries and my sins. But Thou hast brought me nigh—Amen.

E. B. Pusey.

Set my heart on fire with the love of Thee, most loving Father, and then to do Thy will, and to obey Thy commandments, will not be grievous to me. For to him that loveth, nothing is difficult, nothing is impossible; because love is stronger than death. Oh, may love fill and rule my heart. For then there will spring up and be cherished between Thee and me a likeness of character, and union of will, so that I may choose and refuse what Thou dost. May Thy will be done in me and by me forever—Amen.

Paradise for the Christian Soul.

Most merciful God, the helper of all men, so strengthen us by Thy power, that our sorrow may be turned into joy, and we may continually glorify Thy holy Name; through Jesus Christ our Lord—Amen.

Sarum Breviary, A. D. 1085.

June the Twenty-fifth ✦ ✦ ✦ ✦ ✦ 177

O Lord, our Guide even unto death, grant us, I pray Thee, grace to follow Thee whithersoever Thou goest. In little daily duties to which Thou callest us, bow down our wills to simple obedience, patience under pain or provocation, strict truthfulness of word and manner, humility, kindness: in great acts of duty or perfection if Thou shouldest call us to them, uplift us to self-sacrifice, heroic courage, laying down of life for Thy Truth's sake or for a brother—Amen.

Christina G. Rossetti.

O God, the Might of all them that put their trust in Thee, grant that we may be more than conquerors over all that make war upon our souls, and, in the end, may enter into perfect peace in Thy presence —Amen.

Roman Breviary.

June the Twenty-sixth

Lord, do Thou turn me all into love, and all my love into obedience, and let my obedience be without interruption; and then I hope Thou wilt accept such a return as I can make. Make me to be something that Thou delightest in, and Thou shalt have all that I am or have from Thee, even whatsoever Thou makest fit for Thyself—Amen.

Jeremy Taylor (1613-1667).

Almighty and everlasting God, from whom cometh every good and perfect gift, mercifully grant that the frequent meditation of Thine infinite goodness may make us to love Thee above all things; that we may here steadfastly believe what we do not see, and, hereafter, in the blessed vision of Thy glory, see what we now cannot comprehend; through Jesus Christ our Lord—Amen.

Book of Hours, 1865.

June the Twenty-seventh ✠ ✠ ✠ 179

God, the Redeemer of our souls, and the Comforter of them that mourn, whose will is our peace, and to whom obedience is true freedom; grant me so to be led by Thy Holy Spirit, that I may be free from vain hopes and repinings, and from all wrong desires; but may I through patience have experience, and through experience hope, and not be ashamed of hoping in Thee, our Father and our Friend, whose holy will be done now and for ever—Amen.

Rowland Williams.

Lord, renew our spirits and draw our hearts unto Thyself that our work may not be to us a burden, but a delight; and give us such a mighty love to Thee as may sweeten all our obedience. Oh, let us not serve Thee with the spirit of bondage as slaves, but with the cheerfulness and gladness of children, delighting ourselves in Thee and rejoicing in Thy work—Amen.

Benjamin Jenks (1646-1724).

O Thou, who art the true Sun of the world, evermore rising, and never going down; who, by Thy most wholesome appearing and sight dost nourish, and make joyful all things, as well that are in heaven, as also that are on earth; we beseech Thee mercifully and favorably to shine into our hearts, that the night and darkness of sin, and the mists of error on every side, being driven away, Thou brightly shining within our hearts, we may all our life long go without any stumbling or offence, and may walk as in the day-time, being pure and clean from the works of darkness, and abounding in all good works which Thou hast prepared for us to walk in—Amen.

Erasmus (1467-1536).

June the Twenty-ninth ✦ ✦ ✦ ✦ 181

God, Thou only Refuge of Thy children! who remainest true though all else should fail, and livest though all things die, cover us now when we fly to Thee. Rebuke within us all immoderate desires, all unquiet temper, all presumptuous expectations, all ignoble self-indulgence: and feeling on us the embrace of Thy Fatherly hand, may we meekly and with courage go into the darkest ways of our pilgrimage; anxious not to change Thy perfect will, but only to do and bear it worthily. May we spend all our days as in Thy presence, and meet our death in the strength of Thy promise, and pass hence into the nearer light of Thy knowledge and Thy love—Amen.

James Martineau.

182 ✛ ✛ ✛ ✛ ✛ ✛ June the Thirtieth

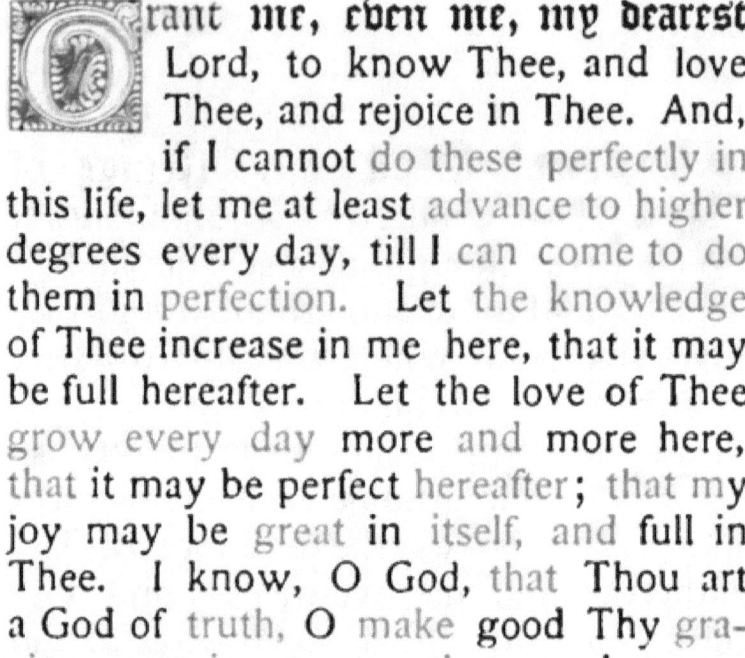

Grant me, even me, my dearest Lord, to know Thee, and love Thee, and rejoice in Thee. And, if I cannot do these perfectly in this life, let me at least advance to higher degrees every day, till I can come to do them in perfection. Let the knowledge of Thee increase in me here, that it may be full hereafter. Let the love of Thee grow every day more and more here, that it may be perfect hereafter; that my joy may be great in itself, and full in Thee. I know, O God, that Thou art a God of truth, O make good Thy gracious promises to me, that my joy may be full—Amen.

St. Augustine (354-430).

 Lord, give us all grace, by constant obedience to offer up our wills and hearts an acceptable sacrifice unto Thee—Amen.

Christina G. Rossetti.

July the First ✤ ✤ ✤ ✤ ✤ ✤ ✤ ✤ 183

Lord, who hast brought us through the darkness of night to the light of the morning, and who by Thy Holy Spirit dost illumine the darkness of ignorance and sin; we beseech Thee, of Thy lovingkindness, to pour Thy holy light into our souls, that we may ever be devoted to Thee by whose wisdom we were created, by whose mercy we were redeemed, and by whose Providence we are governed—Amen.

Book of Hours, 1865.

O God, Fountain of love, pour Thy love into our souls, that we may love those whom Thou lovest, with the love Thou givest us, and think and speak of them tenderly, meekly, lovingly; and so loving our brethren and sisters for Thy sake, may grow in Thy love, and dwelling in love may dwell in Thee; for Jesus Christ's sake—Amen.

E. B. Pusey.

July the Second

 O Heavenly Father, subdue in me whatever is contrary to Thy holy will. Grant that I may ever study to know Thy will, that I may know how to please Thee.

Grant, O God, that I may never run into those temptations, which in my prayers I desire to avoid.

Lord, never permit my trials to be above my strength—Amen.

Thomas Wilson (1663-1755).

O Lord, who delightest in mercy, preserve us, we beseech Thee, from the sin of harboring in our hearts hard thoughts of Thee. Conform us wholly to Thy merciful will; that whether we live we may live unto Thee, or whether we die we may die unto Thee. While we live, give us grace to show mercy: when we die, of Thy grace show us mercy—Amen.

Christina G. Rossetti.

July the Third ✦ ✦ ✦ ✦ ✦ ✦ ✦ ✦ ✦ 185

O God, who hast given unto us Thy Son to be an example and a help to our weakness in following the path that leadeth unto life, grant us so to be His disciples that we may tread in His footsteps—Amen.

Roman Breviary.

O God, grant unto us that we be not unwise, but understanding Thy will: not slothful, but diligent in Thy work : that we run not as uncertainly, nor fight Thy battles as those that beat the air. Whatsoever our hand findeth to do, may we do it with our might: that when Thou shalt call Thy laborers to give them their reward, we may so have run that we may obtain; so have fought the good fight, as to receive the crown of eternal life; through Jesus Christ our Lord—Amen

Henry Alford.

July the Fourth

O God, who art, and wast, and art to come, before whose face the generations rise and pass away; age after age the living seek Thee, and find that of Thy faithfulness there is no end. Our fathers in their pilgrimage walked by Thy guidance, and rested on Thy compassion: still to their children be Thou the cloud by day, the fire by night. In our manifold temptations, Thou alone knowest and art ever nigh: in sorrow, Thy pity revives the fainting soul: in our prosperity and ease, it is Thy Spirit only that can wean us from our pride and keep us low. O Thou sole Source of peace and righteousness! take now the veil from every heart; and join us in one communion with Thy prophets and saints who have trusted in Thee, and were not ashamed. Not of our worthiness, but of Thy tender mercy, hear our prayer— Amen.

James Martineau.

July the Fifth ✢ ✢ ✢ ✢ ✢ ✢ ✢ ✢ 187

God our Father, help us to a deeper trust in the life everlasting. May we feel that this love which is now, ever shall be; this robe of the flesh is Thy gift to Thy child, and, when it is worn out, Thou wilt clothe him again; this work of life is the work Thou hast given us to do, and, when it is done, Thou wilt give us more; this love, that makes all our life so glad, flows from Thee, for Thou art Love, and we shall love forever. Help us to feel how, day by day, we see some dim shadow of the eternal day that will break upon us at the last. May the Gospel of Thy Son, the whisper of Thy Spirit, unite to make our faith in the life to come, strong and clear; then shall we be glad when Thou shalt call us, and enter into Thy glory in Jesus Christ—Amen.

Robert Collyer.

 Merciful Lord, enlighten Thou me with a clear shining inward light, and remove away all darkness from the habitation of my heart. Repress Thou my many wandering thoughts, and break in pieces those temptations which violently assault me. Fight Thou for me, and vanquish the evil beasts; that so peace may be obtained by Thy power, and that Thine abundant praise may resound in Thy holy court, that is, in a pure conscience. Send out Thy light and Thy truth, that they may shine upon the earth; for, until Thou enlighten me, I am but as earth without form and void. Lift Thou up my mind which is pressed down by a load of sins, for no created thing can give full comfort and rest to my desires. Join Thou me to Thyself with an inseparable band of love; for Thou even alone dost satisfy him that loveth Thee—Amen.

Thomas à Kempis.

July the Seventh ✦ ✦ ✦ ✦ ✦ ✦ ✦ 189

Almighty God, the Everlasting Lord, and Giver of every good and perfect gift,—bestow upon us at this time those things that are Thine, even joy and gladness, for Thou art ever-blessed. Pity and pardon us that we are so little able to be like Thee in these things; for upon us are the stains of sin and the dust of earth, the signs of strife and the marks of passion. Look upon us of Thy love, that these things may be taken away, and that we who have been sick in soul, and ofttimes faint in faith, may through the gift of Thine exceeding gladness rise to Thy joy. Forgive our sins, and so take away the sting of death. Grant us Thy love here as the earnest of the Spirit, that we, receiving of Thine in this mortal state, may hope to receive of Thine in the world which is to come—Amen.

George Dawson.

July the Eighth

Be Thou, O Lord, our protection, who art our redemption; direct our minds by Thy gracious presence, and watch over our paths with guiding love; that, among the snares which lie hidden in this path wherein we walk, we may so pass onward with hearts fixed on Thee, that by the track of faith we may come to be where Thou wouldest have us—Amen.

Mozarabic before A. D. 700.

O Lord, make me love every token of Thy will, for love of Thee, and make me cheerful under every cross; take from me all which displeases Thee, or hinders Thy love in me, that I may deeply love Thee. Melt me with Thy love, that I may be all love, and with my whole being love Thee—Amen.

E. B. Pusey.

July the Ninth — 191

Grant, O Lord, that we may carefully watch over our tempers and every unholy feeling; remove whatever in us may be a stumbling-block in another's way; that, by conforming to Thy will in small things, we may hope by Thy protection and help to pass safely through the greater dangers and trials to which we may be exposed—Amen.

Christina G. Rossetti.

We beseech Thee, O Lord, to renew Thy people inwardly and outwardly, that as Thou wouldest not have them to be hindered by bodily pleasures, Thou mayest make them vigorous with spiritual purpose; and refresh them in such sort by things transitory, that Thou mayest grant them rather to cleave to things eternal; through Jesus Christ our Lord—Amen.

Leonine, A. D. 440.

Let Thy love so warm our souls, O Lord, that we may gladly surrender ourselves with all we are and have unto Thee. Let Thy love fall as fire from heaven upon the altar of our hearts; teach us to guard it heedfully by continual devotion and quietness of mind, and to cherish with anxious care every spark of its holy flame with which Thy good Spirit would quicken us, so that neither height, nor depth, things present nor things to come, may ever separate us therefrom. Strengthen Thou our souls; awaken us from the deathly sleep which holds us captive; animate our cold hearts with Thy warmth and tenderness, that we may no more live as in a dream, but walk before Thee as pilgrims in earnest to reach their home. And grant us all at last to meet with Thy holy saints before Thy throne, and there rejoice in Thy love for ever and ever—Amen.

Gerhard Tersteegen, 1731.

July the Eleventh + + + + + + + 193

We confess unto Thee, O God, how weak we are in ourselves, how powerless to do the work of life, how prone to selfishness and sin. We beseech Thee to grant us strength, the strength of Thy Spirit, the power of Thy Christ, wherein we can do all things. Enable us thus to repress every selfish propensity, every wilful purpose, every unkind feeling, every thought and word and deed of anger and impatience, and to cherish perfect love, constant kindness, to think pure thoughts, to speak gentle words, to do helpful and generous deeds. Raise our minds to the contemplation of Thy beloved Son, that, seeing His divine beauty, we may be drawn near unto Him, and changed into His image, and empowered to bring every thought into obedience to Christ, into harmony with His Spirit and His immortal life—Amen.

Thomas C. Stone.

194 ✠ ✠ ✠ ✠ ✠ ✠ ✠ July the Twelfth

Lord, our heavenly Father, who orderest all things for our eternal good, mercifully enlighten our minds, and give us a firm and abiding trust in Thy love and care. Silence our murmurings, quiet our fears, and dispel our doubts, that rising above our afflictions and our anxieties, we may rest on Thee, the Rock of everlasting strength—Amen.

New Church Book of Worship, 1876.

Lord God, King of heaven and earth, may it please Thee this day to order and to hallow, to rule and to govern our hearts and our bodies, our thoughts, our words, and our works, according to Thy commandments, that we, being helped by Thee, may here, and for ever and ever, be delivered and saved, through Jesus Christ our Lord—Amen.

Roman Breviary.

July the Thirteenth ✦ ✦ ✦ ✦ ✦ ✦ 195

O God, who art the unsearchable abyss of peace, the ineffable sea of love, the fountain of blessings, and the bestower of affection, who sendest peace to those that receive it; open to us this day the sea of Thy love, and water us with plenteous streams from the riches of Thy grace. Make us children of quietness, and heirs of peace. Enkindle in us the fire of Thy love; strengthen our weakness by Thy power: bind us closely to Thee and to each other in one firm and indissoluble bond of unity —Amen.

Syrian Clementine Liturgy.

Lord, help us, we entreat Thee, to shew forth our love of Thee by keeping Thy commandments. They are not grievous : remove far from us a repining spirit, an unloving fear to transgress, and all wilful disobedience—Amen.

Christina G. Rossetti.

Thou holy and unspeakable, Thou wonderful and mighty God, whose power and wisdom hath no end, before whom all powers tremble, at whose glance the heavens and the earth flee away, Thou art Love, Thou art my Father, and I will love and worship Thee for ever and ever!

Thou hast deigned to show pity on me, and a ray from Thy light hath shone upon mine inward eye. Guide me on into the perfect light, that it may illumine me wholly, and that all darkness may flee away. Let the holy flame of Thy love so burn in my heart that it be made pure, and I may see Thee, O God; for it is the pure in heart who see Thee. Thou hast set me free; Thou hast drawn me to Thee; therefore forsake me not, but keep me always in Thy grace. Guide me, and rule me, and perfect me for Thy kingdom—Amen.

St. Augustine (354-430).

July the Fifteenth ✦ ✦ ✦ ✦ ✦ ✦ ✦

Holy Spirit, I thirst for Thee, as in a dry, parched land; I pant for the streams of Thy grace. How could I thirst for Thee if Thou wert not the Spirit of my Father? How could I desire Thee, if there were not already in me the same nature as Thine? It is by my need of Thee, that I know my kinship with Thee, with my Father. I have no argument but my need, no language but my cry. I ask for Thee because I require Thee, and I require Thee because I was made for Thee. The prayer that beats against the doors of Thy heaven is the protest of my unfinished nature against its own incompleteness; I shall only be complete in Thee. Come therefore, and finish Thy divine creation. Thou satisfiest the want of every living thing just because its need gives it a right to live; shall not my thirst for Thee, O Spirit of holiness, give me also a right to the river of Thy pleasures?—Amen.

George Matheson.

The Lord be my Keeper, the Lord be my Defence upon my right hand. The Lord preserve me from all evil, yea, the Lord keep my soul. The Lord preserve my going out, and my coming in, from this time forth for evermore.

O Lord! Thou knowest, Thou art able, Thou art willing, to do good to my soul; I neither know how, nor am able, nor, as I ought, willing to do it.

Do Thou, O Lord, I beseech Thee, in Thine unspeakable loving-kindness, so order and dispose of me as Thou knowest to be best pleasing to Thee, and most expedient for me.

Thine are goodness, grace, love, kindness, O Thou Lover of men! gentleness, tenderness, forbearance, long-suffering, manifold mercies, great mercies, abundant tender compassions. Glory be to Thee, O Lord—Amen.

Lancelot Andrewes (1555-1626).

July the Seventeenth ✛ ✛ ✛ ✛ ✛ 199

Though we know not what is best, give to us, Lord, what Thou seest fit; only fit us for what Thou givest, and let it bring to our souls health and peace, with some good to our neighbor and the world, for Thy goodness' sake, O Lord.

Make me to Thyself a temple of holy things, and abiding with me, O Lord, at the last, be ever gracious unto Thy servant.

Let me do some work which may be accepted in Thy mercy, though unworthy in Thy pure sight.

Bless my work to good, to the fulness of which it is capable, and let me thank Thee for it with joy in the end.

Into Thy hands we commend our spirit, soul, and body, of which Thou art Creator, Saviour, Restorer, a God of truth.

Lord, to Thee I commit my going out and my coming in this day—Amen.

Rowland Williams.

Hallowed be Thy name. Supported by faith in Thee, I shall stand steadfast and secure under every cross, tribulation, distress, disease, and even death itself; nothing doubting either Thy divine power or Thy Fatherly love whereby Thou art both able and willing to preserve me. Call me hence whensoever Thou wilt, but grant that I may follow cheerfully, firmly believing that Thou art mighty and good; then shall Thy loving Spirit lead me forth into the land of uprightness. Thy will be done on earth, as it is in heaven. And what is Thy will, O most loving Father, except that I should love Thee? Behold, Thou commandest that I should love Thee with all my heart and soul, with all my mind and strength; but grant Thou me what Thou commandest, and command what Thou wilt —Amen.

Paradise for the Christian Soul.

July the Nineteenth — 201

"What shall I render unto Him for all His benefits?" I can only give my own self—all I have, and all I am. I desire to surrender myself wholly unto Thee, O my God, to live more simply as one separated unto Thee, not finding my joy and comfort in the earthly blessings Thou so richly bestowest on me, but, while thankful for the gracious gifts, looking only to the Giver as the Source of my happiness and the Object of my life. I cannot shake off the habits of thought and feeling which many years have wrought in me; I can only ask of Thee to have mercy on me, poor and needy as I am, and subdue in me all that is perverse and wayward in my heart, and so fill me with Thy pure and heavenly love, that all my narrowness and selfishness may be done away in the wideness of Thy love—Amen.

Maria Hare.

July the Twentieth

Most glorious God! relieve my spirit with Thy graciousness; take from me all tediousness of spirit, and give me a hope that shall not fail, a desire of holiness not to be satisfied till it possesses a charity that will always increase; that I may turn all things into religion, doing all to Thy glory; that, when Thou shalt call me from this deliciousness of employment, I may pass into the employments of saints and angels; whose work it is, with eternal joy and thanksgiving, to sing praises unto Thy mercies—Amen.

Jeremy Taylor (1613-1667).

Almighty God, grant, we beseech Thee, that we whose trust is under the shadow of Thy wings, may, through the help of Thy power, overcome all evils that rise up against us—Amen.

Roman Breviary.

July the Twenty-first 203

O Thou Almighty Helper and ever-present God, we bring to Thee all our needs. O Thou Author of all good, from whom cometh every good and perfect gift, may Thy mercies be our daily song, and may the light of Thy countenance in this world of power and beauty move our hearts to great thankfulness and a sweet trust. Day by day Thou dost appoint our portion, especially revealing Thy glory in the dear Son of Thy love, and calling us into His Kingdom of service and blessedness. May this be our love of Thee in Him, that we love one another and keep all His commandments—Amen.

Rufus Ellis.

We beseech Thee, O Lord, to keep us in perpetual peace, as Thou hast vouchsafed us confidence in Thee; through Jesus Christ our Lord—Amen.

Gelasian Sacramentary, A. D. 492.

July the Twenty-second

Eternal Father, help me, I beseech Thee, to bring forth in my life the fruits of the Spirit; the fruit of Love, that I may love Thee above all things, and all others in Thee and for Thy sake; the fruit of Joy, that I may find Thy service my delight; the fruit of Peace, that, pardoned and accepted through Thy mercy, I may repose in Thy love; the fruit of Long-suffering, that I may bear, with patient submission to Thy will, all crosses and afflictions; the fruit of Gentleness, that I may subdue all risings of temper, and take calmly and sweetly all trials and provocations; the fruit of Meekness, that I may forgive freely all who may hurt me either by word or deed, and endure with patience all that may be laid upon me; the fruit of Temperance that I may restrain all my desires, bringing them into subjection in all things to Thy holy will—Amen.

Treasury of Devotion, 1869.

July the Twenty-third ✦ ✦ ✦ ✦ ✦ 205

Almighty God, who canst give the light that in darkness shall make us glad, the life that in gloom shall make us joy, and the peace that amidst discord shall bring us quietness! let us live this day in that light, that life, and that peace, so that we may gain the victory over those things that press us down, and over the flesh that so often encumbers us, and over death that seemeth for a moment to win the victory. Thus we, being filled with inward peace, and light, and life, may walk all the days of this our mortal life, doing our work as the business of our Father, glorifying it, because it is Thy will, knowing that what Thou givest Thou givest in love. Bestow upon us the greatest and last blessing, that we, being in Thy presence, may be like unto Thee for evermore. These things we do ask, in the name of Jesus Christ our Lord —Amen.

George Dawson.

July the Twenty-fourth

O Lord of heaven and earth, we are truly sorry for all our misdoings; we utterly renounce whatsoever is contrary to Thy will, and here devote ourselves entirely to the obedience thereof. Accept, O most merciful Father, of this renewed dedication which we make of ourselves, our bodies, souls, and spirits unto Thee. And grant that we may be able every day to offer up ourselves more sincerely, and more cheerfully unto Thee; with more pure affection, and hearty devotion, and ready disposition to Thy service. Preserve in our minds a grateful sense of Thy mighty love, that we may follow the doctrine and example of Thy Son Jesus Christ. Grant that we may be like Him, pure and undefiled, meek and gentle, peaceable and patient, contented and thankful. Fulfil unto us all the gracious promises that He hath made unto us. Let it be unto Thy servants according to His word—Amen.

Simon Patrick (1626-1707).

July the Twenty-fifth

Lord, shew forth Thy loving-kindness, I entreat Thee, to all persons who in this world feel themselves neglected, or little loved, or forgotten. Be Thou their beloved Companion, and let communion with Thee be to them more dear than tenderest earthly intercourse. Teach them to discern Thee in all with whom they come in contact, and to love and serve Thee in them. On earth grant them comfort by the repentance of any who have wronged them, and in heaven comfort in the communion of all saints with each other and with Thee—Amen.

Christina G. Rossetti.

✥

Gracious Lord, who apprehendest the sighing of a contrite heart before it be uttered; make us, we beseech Thee, the temple of the Holy Spirit, that we may be defended by the shield of Thy celestial goodness, through Christ our Lord—Amen.

Sarum Breviary, A. D. 1085.

July the Twenty-sixth

O Lord, in whose hands are life and death, by whose power I am sustained, and by whose mercy I am spared, look down upon me with pity. Forgive me that I have until now so much neglected the duty which Thou hast assigned to me, and suffered the days and hours of which I must give account to pass away without any endeavor to accomplish Thy will. Make me to remember, O God, that every day is Thy gift, and ought to be used according to Thy command. Grant me, therefore, so to repent of my negligence, that I may obtain mercy from Thee, and pass the time which Thou shalt yet allow me in diligent performance of Thy commands, through Jesus Christ—Amen.

Samuel Johnson (1709-1784).

Thou Eternal, in whose appointment our life standeth! Thou hast committed our work to us, and we would commit our cares to Thee. May we feel that we are not our own, and that Thou wilt heed our wants, while we are intent upon Thy will. May we never dwell carelessly or say in our hearts, "I am here, and there is none over me"; nor anxiously, as though our path were hid; but with a mind simply fixed upon our trust, and choosing nothing but the dispositions of Thy Providence. More and more fill us with that pity for others' troubles which comes from forgetfulness of our own; and the glad hope of the children of eternity. And unto Thee, the Beginning and the End, Lord of the living, Refuge of the dying, be thanks and praise for ever!—Amen.

James Martineau.

Lord, what is my confidence which I have in this life? Is it not Thou, O Lord, my God, whose mercies are without number? Where hath it ever been well with me without Thee, or where could it be ill with me, when Thou wert present? I rather choose to be a pilgrim on earth, than without Thee to possess heaven. Where Thou art, there is heaven; and where Thou art not, there is death and hell. There is none that can help me in my necessities, but only Thou, my God; Thou art my Hope, Thou my Confidence. Although Thou exposest me to divers temptations and adversities, yet Thou orderest all this to my advantage; in which trial of me Thou oughtest no less to be loved and praised, than if Thou didst fill me full of heavenly consolations—Amen.

Thomas à Kempis.

July the Twenty-ninth ✦ ✦ ✦ ✦ 211

My God, my whole life has been a course of mercies and blessings shown to one who has been most unworthy of them. Year after year Thou hast carried me on, removed dangers from my path, refreshed me, borne with me, directed me, sustained me. O forsake me not, when my strength faileth me. And Thou never wilt forsake me. I may securely repose upon Thee. While I am true to Thee, Thou wilt still, and to the end, be superabundantly good to me. I may rest upon Thy arm; I may go to sleep in Thy bosom. Only give me, and increase in me, that true loyalty to Thee, which is the bond of the covenant between Thee and me, and the pledge in my own heart and conscience that Thou, the Supreme God, wilt not forsake me—Amen.

John Henry Newman.

July the Thirtieth

Thou loving and tender Father in heaven, I confess before Thee, in deep sorrow, how hard and unsympathizing is my heart; how often I have sinned against my neighbor by want of compassion and tenderness; how often I have felt no true pity for his trials and sorrows, and have neglected to comfort, help, and visit him. O Father, forgive this heavy sin, and lay it not to my charge. Give me grace ever to alleviate the crosses and difficulties of those around me, and never to add to them; teach me to be a consoler in sorrow, to take thought for the stranger, the widow, and the orphan; let my charity show itself not in words only but in deed and truth. Teach me to judge, as Thou dost, with forbearance, with much pity and indulgence; and help me to avoid all unloving judgment of others—Amen.

Johann Arndt (1555-1621).

July the Thirty-first — 213

Bestow Thy light upon us, O Lord, so that, being rid of the darkness of our hearts, we may attain unto the true light—Amen.

Sarum Breviary, A. D. 1085.

Almighty God, who forgivest all things to those who cry unto Thee, grant unto us that, whatsoever of life there may be remaining for us, we may give diligent heed at this very hour to Thy call; that, so coming unto Thee, we may find work in Thy vineyard, and do it faithfully unto the end; beseeching Thee to forgive the wasted hours of the past, and of Thy graciousness to see that there be no more. For all time to come grant us to serve Thee diligently and dutifully, that at last we may hear Thy voice saying unto us, "Well done, good and faithful servants: enter ye into the joy of your Lord." So be it unto us all, through Jesus Christ our Lord—Amen.

George Dawson.

Almighty and eternal God, there is no number of Thy days or of Thy mercies: Thou hast sent us into this world to serve Thee, and to live according to Thy laws. O dear Lord, look upon us in mercy and pity: let Thy Holy Spirit lead us through this world with safety and peace, with holiness and religion, with spiritual comforts and joy in the Holy Ghost; that when we have served Thee in our generation, we may be gathered unto our fathers, having the testimony of a holy conscience, in the confidence of a certain faith, and the comforts of a reasonable, religious, and holy hope, and perfect charity with Thee our God and all the world; that neither death nor life, nor angels nor principalities, nor powers, nor things present, nor things to come, nor height, nor depth, nor any other creature, may be able to separate us from the love of God, which is in Christ Jesus our Lord—Amen.

Jeremy Taylor (1613-1667).

August the Second — 215

Lord, I thank Thee that Thy love constraineth me. I thank Thee that, in the great labyrinth of life, Thou waitest not for my consent to lead me. I thank Thee that Thou leadest me by a way which I know not, by a way which is above the level of my poor understanding. I thank Thee that Thou art not repelled by my bitterness, that Thou art not turned aside by the heat of my spirit. There is no force in this universe so glorious as the force of Thy love; it compels me to come in. O divine servitude, O slavery that makes me free, O love that imprisons me only to set my feet in a larger room, enclose me more and more within Thy folds. Protect me from the impetuous desires of my nature—desires as short-lived as they are impetuous. Ask me not where I would like to go; tell me where to go; lead me in Thine own way; hold me in Thine own light—Amen.

George Matheson.

August the Third

God, our heavenly Father, who hast commanded us to love one another as Thy children, and hast ordained the highest friendship in the bond of Thy Spirit, we beseech Thee to maintain and preserve us always in the same bond, to Thy glory, and our mutual comfort, with all those to whom we are bound by any special tie, either of nature or of choice; that we may be perfected together in that love which is from above, and which never faileth when all other things shall fail. Send down the dew of Thy heavenly grace upon us, that we may have joy in each other that passeth not away; and, having lived together in love here, according to Thy commandment, may live for ever together with them, being made one in Thee, in Thy glorious kingdom hereafter, through Jesus Christ our Lord—Amen.

Hickes' Devotions, 1700.

August the Fourth ✢ ✢ ✢ ✢ ✢ ✢ 217

Lord, what cross willest Thou that I should bear this day, for love of Thee? Thou knowest. Lord, that I am all weakness, strengthen me to bear it patiently, humbly, lovingly. If I sink under it, look on me and raise me up. Give what Thou commandest, and command what Thou wilt; sanctify my cross to me, and keep me Thine own for ever—Amen.

E. B. Pusey.

God, the Protector of all that trust in Thee, without whom nothing is strong, nothing is holy, increase and multiply upon us Thy mercy; that, Thou being our Ruler and Guide, we may so pass through things temporal that we finally lose not the things eternal. Grant this, O heavenly Father, for Jesus Christ's sake our Lord—Amen.

Gregorian, A. D. 590.

218 ✢ ✢ ✢ ✢ ✢ ✢ ✢ August the Fifth

O God of strength, passing all understanding, who mercifully givest to Thy people mercy and judgment; grant to us, we beseech Thee, faithfully to love Thee, and to walk in the way of righteousness—Amen.

Sarum Breviary, A. D. 1085.

O Lord, Shield of our help, who wilt not suffer us to be tempted above that we are able, help us, we entreat Thee, in all our straits and wrestlings, to lift up our eyes unto Thee, and stay our hearts on Thee—Amen.

Christina G. Rossetti.

O God, the Father of mercies, grant unto us ever to hold fast to the spirit of adoption, whereby we cry to Thee, "Father," and are called, and are, Thy sons; through our Lord Jesus Christ—Amen.

Roman Breviary.

My Lord, in Thine arms I am safe; keep me and I have nothing to fear; give me up, and I have nothing to hope for. I know nothing about the future, but I rely upon Thee. I pray Thee to give me what is good for me; I pray Thee to take from me whatever may imperil my salvation. I leave it all to Thee, because Thou knowest and I do not. If Thou bringest pain or sorrow on me, give me grace to bear it well, keep me from fretfulness and selfishness. If Thou givest me health and strength and success in this world, keep me ever on my guard lest these great gifts carry me away from Thee. Give me to know Thee, to believe on Thee, to love Thee, to serve Thee, to live to and for Thee. Give me to die just at that time and in that way which is most for Thy glory—Amen.

John Henry Newman.

Blessed art Thou, O Lord our God, the God of our fathers, who turnest the shadow of death into the morning; who hast lightened mine eyes, that I sleep not in death. O Lord, blot out as a night-mist mine iniquities. Scatter my sins as a morning cloud. Grant that I may become a child of the light, and of the day. Vouchsafe to keep me this day without sin. Uphold me when I am falling, and lift me up when I am down. Preserve this day from any evil of mine, and me from the evils of the day. Let this day add some knowledge, or good deed, to yesterday. Oh, let me hear Thy lovingkindness in the morning, for in Thee is my trust. Teach me to do the thing that pleaseth Thee, for Thou art my God. Let Thy loving Spirit lead me forth into the land of righteousness—Amen.

Lancelot Andrewes (1555-1626).

August the Eighth ✦ ✦ ✦ ✦ ✦ ✦ ✦ 221

Let all Thy works praise Thee, O Lord, and Thy servants rejoice in thanking Thee. True is Thy word, which counts us worthy of pity, and faithful Thy help for our heart's trust to rest upon. O God, Thy strength is made perfect in those who have not cared for themselves, but sought the eternal; then Thou bringest forth truth to victory. Make known to me Thy ways, O God, and let me walk in Thy truth. Go on, O God, victoriously, and open me the gate of hope, out of darkness into light. Since Thou hast not taken me away in the midst of my day, but upholden my soul in life, suffer not my feet to slip. Grant me a work of Thy love to do, and prosper it in my hands. Let me not die until I have fulfilled Thy will; and let me enter with joy into rest—Amen.

Rowland Williams.

Thee, most merciful God, do I now invoke to descend into my soul, which Thou hast prepared for Thy reception by the desire which Thou hast breathed into it. Ere ever I cried to Thee, Thou, most Merciful, hadst called and sought me, that I might find Thee, and finding love Thee. Even so I sought and found Thee, Lord, and desire to love Thee. Increase my desire, and grant me what I ask. See, I love Thee, but too little; strengthen my love. When my spirit aspires to Thee, and meditates on Thine unspeakable goodness, the burden of the flesh becomes less heavy, the tumult of thought is stilled, the weight of mortality is less oppressive. Then fain would my soul find wings, that she might rise in tireless flight ever upwards to Thy glorious throne, and there be filled with the refreshing solace that belongs to the citizens of heaven—Amen.

St. Augustine (354–430).

August the Tenth ✦ ✦ ✦ ✦ ✦ ✦ ✦

O Sovereign and Almighty Lord, bless all Thy people, and all Thy flock. Give Thy peace, Thy help, Thy love unto us Thy servants, the sheep of Thy fold, that we may be united in the bond of peace and love, one body and one spirit, in one hope of our calling, in Thy divine and boundless love—Amen.

Liturgy of St. Mark (175–234?).

Almighty God, Giver of life, grant unto us Thy life, that we may truly live; Thy love, that we may greatly rejoice; that we, knowing trouble, and acquainted with grief, may, through the goodly deliverance of faith and hope, come to the large joy of the peace that passeth all understanding. Of Thy loving-kindness hear our supplications, we beseech Thee, through Jesus Christ our Lord—Amen.

George Dawson.

Show Thy mercy to me, O Lord, to glad my heart withal. Let me find Thee, for whom I long. Lo, here the man that was caught of thieves, wounded, and left for half dead, as he was going towards Jericho. Thou kind-hearted Samaritan, take me up. I am the sheep that is gone astray; O good Shepherd, seek me out, and bring me home to Thy fold again. Deal favorably with me according to Thy good pleasure, that I may dwell in Thy house all the days of my life, and praise Thee for ever and ever with them that are there—Amen.

St. Jerome.   Translated A. D. 1578.

O God, the Renewer and Lover of innocency, turn the hearts of all Thy servants to Thyself, that they may be found ever rooted in faith and fruitful in works, through Jesus Christ our Lord—Amen.

Sarum Breviary, A. D. 1085.

August the Twelfth ✦ ✦ ✦ ✦ ✦ ✦

 Lord, our Hiding-place, grant us wisdom, we pray Thee, to seek no hiding-place out of Thee in life or in death. Now hide us in Thine own Presence from the provoking of all men, and keep us from the strife of tongues. Make us meek, humble, patient, and teach us to seek peace and ensue it—Amen.

Christina G. Rossetti.

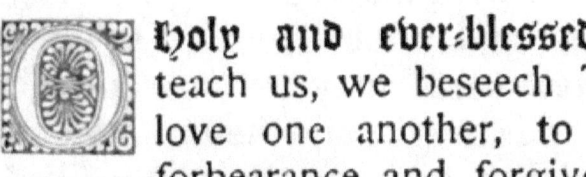 Holy and ever-blessed Lord, teach us, we beseech Thee, to love one another, to exercise forbearance and forgiveness towards our enemies; to recompense no man evil for evil, but to be merciful even as Thou, our Father in Heaven, art merciful: that so we may continually follow after Thee in all our doings, and be more and more conformed to Thine image and likeness—Amen.

New Church Book of Worship, 1876.

Lord, we acknowledge Thy dominion over us; our life, our death, our soul and body, all belong to Thee. Oh, grant that we may willingly consecrate them all to Thee, and use them in Thy service. Let us walk before Thee in childlike simplicity, steadfast in prayer; looking ever unto Thee, that whatsoever we do or abstain from we may in all things follow the least indications of Thy will. Become Lord of our hearts and spirits; that the whole inner man may be brought under Thy rule, and that Thy life of love and righteousness may pervade all our thoughts and energies and the very ground of our souls; that we may be wholly filled with it. Come, O Lord and King, enter into our hearts, and live and reign there for ever and ever. O faithful Lord, teach us to trust Thee for life and death, and to take Thee for our All in All—Amen.

Gerhard Tersteegen, 1731.

August the Fourteenth ✦ ✦ ✦ ✦ ✦ 227

O Thou, whose name is Love, who never turnest away from the cry of Thy needy children, give ear to my prayer this morning. Make this a day of blessing to me, and make me a blessing to others. Keep all evil away from me. Preserve me from outward transgression and from secret sin. Help me to control my temper. May I check the first risings of anger or sullenness. If I meet with unkindness or ill-treatment, give me that charity which suffereth long and beareth all things. Make me kind and gentle towards all, loving even those who love me not. Let me live this day as if it were to be my last. O my God, show me the path that Thou wouldest have me to follow. May I take no step that is not ordered by Thee, and go nowhere except Thou, Lord, go with me—Amen.

Ashton Oxenden.

Thou most holy and ever-loving God, we thank Thee once more for the quiet rest of the night that has gone by, for the new promise that has come with this fresh morning, and for the hope of this day. While we have slept, the world in which we live has swept on in its awful space, great fires have burned under us, great waters have been all about us, and great storms above us; but Thou hast held them back by Thy strong hand, and we have rested under the shadow of Thy love. The bird sat on the spray out in the darkness, the flower nestled in the grass, we lay down in our home, and all slept in the arms of God. The bird will trust Thee this day to give its morsel of meat, and the flower will trust Thee for its fresh raiment; so may we trust Thee this day for all the needs of the body, the soul, and the spirit. Give us this day our daily bread—Amen.

Robert Collyer.

August the Sixteenth + + + + + 229

Father, this day may bring some hard task to our life, or some hard trial to our love. We may grow weary, or sad, or hopeless in our lot. But, Father, our whole life until now has been one great proof of Thy care. Bread has come for our body, thoughts to our mind, love to our heart, and all from Thee. So help us, we implore Thee, while we stand still on this side of all that the day may bring, to resolve that we will trust Thee this day to shine into any gloom of the mind, to stand by us in any trial of our love, and to give us rest in Thy good time as we need. May this day be full of a power that shall bring us near to Thee, and make us more like Thee; and, O God, may we so trust Thee this day, that, when the day is done, our trust shall be firmer than ever. Then, when our last day comes, and our work is done, may we trust Thee in death and forever, in the spirit of Jesus Christ our Lord—Amen.

Robert Collyer.

August the Seventeenth

Strengthen me, O God, by the grace of Thy Holy Spirit. Grant me to be strengthened with might in the inner man, and to empty my heart of all useless care and anguish. O Lord, grant me heavenly wisdom, that I may learn above all things to seek and to find Thee, above all things to relish and to love Thee, and to think of all other things as being, what indeed they are, at the disposal of Thy wisdom—Amen.

Thomas à Kempis.

Most merciful God, the Foundation of our hope and our Refuge in trouble, deliver us from the snares of death; so that, saved from the multitude of troubles which surround us, we may sing praises to Thy holy Name, in purity and innocence; through our Lord Jesus Christ—Amen.

Sarum Breviary, A. D. 1085.

August the Eighteenth ✦ ✦ ✦ ✦ ✦ 231

O Lord, who spreadest out the heavens like a curtain, give us, we pray Thee, faithful wills and loving hearts, that in all Thy works we may ever discern Thee. O Lord, we humbly bless Thee for what Thou givest, and for what Thou withholdest; for the knowledge Thou bestowest, and for the knowledge Thou keepest back—Amen.

     Christina G. Rossetti.

I Thank Thee, my Creator and Lord, that Thou hast given me these joys in Thy creation, this ecstacy over the works of Thy hands. I have made known the glory of Thy works to men as far as my finite spirit was able to comprehend Thy infinity. If I have said anything wholly unworthy of Thee, or have aspired after my own glory, graciously forgive me—Amen.

    Johann Kepler (1571-1630).

O Lord, grant to us so to love Thee with all our heart, with all our mind, and all our soul, and our neighbor for Thy sake; that the grace of charity and brotherly love may dwell in us, and all envy, harshness, and ill-will may die in us; and fill our hearts with feelings of love, kindness, and compassion, so that, by constantly rejoicing in the happiness and good success of others, by sympathizing with them in their sorrows, and putting away all harsh judgments and envious thoughts, we may follow Thee, who art Thyself the true and perfect Love—Amen.

Treasury of Devotion.

Pour upon us, O Lord, the spirit of brotherly kindness and peace; so that, sprinkled with the dew of Thy benediction, we may be made glad by Thy glory and grace; through Christ our Lord—Amen.

Sarum Breviary, A. D. 1085.

August the Twentieth + + + + + 233

Grant unto us, Almighty God, that that glory which filleth earth and heaven may also fill our hearts; that we, being glorified by Thy graciousness, made happy by Thy love, made hopeful by Thy promise, may praise and magnify Thy holy Name, until such time as the praising of Thy holy Name shall lead us to the doing of Thy holy will; that we, becoming perfectly obedient thereunto, may possess the life of God in the days of time, that so, in the eternal years, we may be for ever Thine. Receive our thanksgivings, forgive our sins, strengthen our hope, make deep our faith; that so, all the days of this our mortal life, we, keeping Thy commandments, and leaning ever upon Thy mercy, may pass on our way until we, through the gate of death, enter into the life everlasting. Hear us of Thy mercy, through Jesus Christ our Lord—Amen.

George Dawson.

August the Twenty-first

Cleanse me, O God, by the bright fountain of Thy mercy, and water me with the dew of Thine abundant grace, that, being purified from my sins, I may grow up in good works, truly serving Thee in holiness and righteousness all the days of my life—Amen.

Private Devotions, 1560.

O God, the God of all goodness and all grace, who art worthy of a greater love than we can either give or understand; fill my heart, I beseech Thee, with such love towards Thee as may cast out all sloth and fear, that nothing may seem too hard for me to do or to suffer in obedience to Thee; and grant that, by thus loving, I may become daily more like unto Thee; and finally obtain the crown of life, which Thou hast promised to those that love Thee; through Jesus Christ our Lord—Amen.

Pocket Manual of Prayers, 1860.

August the Twenty-second + + +235

Lord, I believe, but would believe more firmly; O Lord, I love, but yet would love more warmly.

I offer unto Thee my thoughts, that they may be towards Thee; my deeds, that they may be according to Thee; my sufferings, that they may be for Thee—Amen.

Treasury of Devotion, 1869.

Be not weary of me, good Lord, and let me not be weary of myself, or of trying to conquer myself. I am all weakness, but Thou art almighty, and canst put forth Thy strength perfectly in my weakness. Make me truly to hate all which Thou hatest, fervently to love all which Thou lovest; make me truly sorry, for love of Thee, that I have so often offended Thee, and so mightily transform me, through Thy grace, that I may no more offend Thee; through Jesus Christ—Amen.

E. B. Pusey.

August the Twenty-third

O God our Lord, the stay of all them that put their trust in Thee, wherever Thou leadest we would go, for Thy ways are perfect wisdom and love. Even when we walk through the dark valley, Thy light can shine into our hearts and guide us safely through the night of sorrow. Be Thou our Friend, and we need ask no more in heaven or earth; for Thou art the Comfort of all who trust in Thee, the Help and Defence of all who hope in Thee. O Lord, we would be Thine; let us never fall away from Thee. We would accept all things without murmuring from Thy hand, for whatever Thou dost is right. Blend our wills with Thine, and then we need fear no evil nor death itself, for all things must work together for our good. Lord, keep us in Thy love and truth; comfort us with Thy light; and guide us by Thy Holy Spirit —Amen.

S. Weiss (1738–1805).

August the Twenty-fourth + + +237

O Lord, Strength of our life, be Thou, I entreat Thee, our Strength unto life eternal: our Strength when temptation assails us, for Thou art stronger than our strongest enemy; our Strength when we go down into the valley of the shadow of death, for the last enemy that shall be destroyed is death. By Thy Rod and Thy Staff comfort us—Amen.

Christina G. Rossetti.

We humbly pray Thee, O Father in heaven, to guide us through the darkness of this world, to guard us from its perils, to hold us up and strengthen us when we grow weary in our mortal way; and to lead us by Thy chosen paths, through time and through death, to our eternal home in Thy heavenly kingdom; which we ask in the name of Jesus Christ our Lord—Amen.

King's Chapel Liturgy, 1831.

O Thou ever blessed Fountain of life, I bless Thee that Thou hast infused into me Thine own vital breath, so that I am become a living soul. It is my earnest desire that I may not only live, but grow; grow in grace, and in the knowledge of my Lord and Saviour Jesus Christ. May I grow in patience and fortitude of soul, in humility and zeal, in spirituality and a heavenly disposition of mind. In a word, as Thou knowest I hunger and thirst after righteousness, make me whatever Thou wouldest delight to see me. Draw on my soul, by the gentle influences of Thy gracious Spirit, every trace and every feature which Thine eye, O heavenly Father, may survey with pleasure, and which Thou mayest acknowledge as Thine own image. I ask and hope it through Him of whose fulness we have all received—Amen.

Philip Doddridge (1702-1751).

August the Twenty-sixth + + + 239

O Lord, the Author and Persuader of peace, love, and good-will, soften our hard and steely hearts, warm our icy and frozen hearts, that we may wish well to one another, and may be the true disciples of Jesus Christ. And give us grace even now to begin to show forth that heavenly life, wherein there is no disagreement nor hatred, but peace and love on all hands, one towards another—Amen.

Ludovicus Vives, A. D. 1578.

By that forgiving tenderness, O Lord, wherewith Thou didst ever wait for me; by that tender love wherewith, whenever I wandered, Thou watchest over me; by Thine infinite love, wherewith Thou willest that I should love Thee eternally; give me love like Thine, that I may forgive, compassionate, love like Thee—Amen.

E. B. Pusey.

August the Twenty-seventh

O Lord our God, who hast chased the slumber from our eyes, and once more assembled us to lift up our hands unto Thee, and to praise Thy just judgments, accept our prayers and supplications, and give us faith that maketh not ashamed, confident hope and love unfeigned; bless our coming-in and going-out, our thoughts, words, and works, and let us begin this day with the praise of the unspeakable sweetness of Thy mercy. Hallowed be Thy name; Thy kingdom come—Amen.

Greek Church.

O Lord, who art as the shadow of a great rock in a weary land, who beholdest Thy weak creatures, weary of labor, weary of pleasure, weary of hope deferred, weary of self, in Thine abundant compassion and unutterable tenderness, bring us, we pray Thee, unto Thy rest—Amen.

Christina G. Rossetti.

August the Twenty-eighth

Lord, I fling myself with all my weakness and misery into Thy ever-open arms. I know that I am ignorant and much mistaken about myself. Thou, who seest in very truth, look mercifully on me. Lay Thy healing hand upon my wounds. Pour the life-giving balm of Thy love into my heart. Do for me what I have not the courage to do for myself. Save me in spite of myself. May I be Thine; wholly Thine, and, at all costs, Thine. In humiliation, in poverty, in suffering, in self-abnegation, Thine. Thine in the way Thou knowest to be most fitting, in order that Thou mightest be now and ever mine. Thou art my Strength and my Redeemer. I am Thy poor little creature, dependent on Thy merciful charity alone—Amen.

père Besson (1816–1861).

August the Twenty-ninth

May Thy most holy will be done by me and by all pilgrims here below, in the perfect performance of Thy precepts, and all Thy good pleasure, as readily and constantly all the days and moments of our life on earth, as it is done by the blessed. Out of the boundless treasury of Thy mercy pardon us all the sins we have committed in thought, word, deed, or by omission, against Thee and against our neighbors, as we forgive all their offences. Mercifully preserve and deliver us from all evils both of body and soul, present and to come, so far as they may hold us back in the attainment of perfection; that so we may, without hindrance, more perfectly love and glorify Thee in time, more blessedly hereafter in eternity. May what I ask be done, as Thou wilt, when Thou wilt, how Thou wilt, through Thy tender mercy—Amen.

Father Christ. Mayer.

August the Thirtieth ✦ ✦ ✦ ✦ ✦ 243

 God, who hast in mercy taught us how good it is to follow the holy desires which Thou manifoldly puttest into our hearts, and how bitter is the grief of falling short of whatever beauty our minds behold, strengthen us, we beseech Thee, to walk steadfastly throughout life in the better path which our hearts once chose; and give us wisdom to tread it prudently in Thy fear, as well as cheerfully in Thy love; so that, having been faithful to Thee all the days of our life here, we may be able hopefully to resign ourselves into Thy hands hereafter—Amen.

Rowland Williams.

We beseech Thee, O Lord, let the power of the Holy Spirit be present with us, that it may both mercifully cleanse our hearts, and protect us from all adversities; through our Lord Jesus Christ—Amen.

Leonine Sacramentary, A. D. 440.

O Lord, forasmuch as all my strength is in Thee, grant unto me this grace, that I may allow Thee to do whatsoever Thou wilt; and that my doing may be to lie still in Thy hand, that Thou mayest do with me that thing only which is most pleasing to Thee. Do Thou adorn me with holy virtues, giving unto me humbleness of mind, purity of heart, and all those gifts and graces which Thou knowest to be needful for me, and whatsoever Thou wouldest have to be in me, whether in body or soul; that so I may be able the better to please Thee, the more worthily and faithfully to serve Thee, and the more perfectly to love Thee. I pray, moreover, that Thou wouldest give me grace to arrive at that degree of perfection which Thou willest me to reach, and grant unto me the aids and dispositions needful for its attainment—Amen.

Ludovicus Palma.

September the First ✦ ✦ ✦ ✦ ✦ ✦ 245

O Lord, my God! the amazing horrors of darkness were gathered round me, and covered me all over, and I saw no way to go forth; I felt the depth and extent of the misery of my fellow-creatures separated from the Divine harmony, and it was heavier than I could bear, and I was crushed down under it; I lifted up my hand, I stretched out my arm, but there was none to help me; I looked round about, and was amazed. In the depths of misery, O Lord, I remembered that Thou art omnipotent; that I had called Thee Father; and I felt that I loved Thee, and I was made quiet in my will, and I waited for deliverance from Thee. Thou hadst pity upon me, when no man could help me; I saw that meekness under suffering was showed to us in the most affecting example of Thy Son, and Thou taughtest me to follow Him, and I said, "Thy will, O Father, be done!"

John Woolman (1720–1772).

September the Second

O Lord, give us grace, I pray Thee, so to realize Thine almighty succor pledged to us, Thy protecting Presence surrounding us, Thine all-seeing eye fixed upon us, Thy Divine heart yearning over us, that we may cease to tremble at man's anger, or shrink from man's ridicule; but may with a good courage perform the work Thou givest us to do, and after we have suffered may enter into rest—Amen.

Christina G. Rossetti.

Heavenly Father, the Author and Fountain of all truth, the bottomless Sea of all understanding, send, we beseech Thee, Thy Holy Spirit into our hearts, and lighten our understandings with the beams of Thy heavenly grace. We ask this, O merciful Father, for Thy dear Son, our Saviour, Jesus Christ's sake—Amen.

Nicholas Ridley (1500-1555).

September the Third ✦ ✦ ✦ ✦ ✦ 247

Grant, we beseech Thee, O Lord God, unto all Thy servants, that they may continually enjoy health both of mind and body, may be delivered from present sadness, and enter into the joy of Thine eternal gladness—Amen.

Roman Breviary.

Grant unto us, Almighty God, by Thy good Spirit, that we, feeling towards Thee as children, and filled full of trust, and hope, and faith, may remain so fixed, that, in the dark, we may trust where we cannot see, and hope where all seems doubtful, ever looking unto Thee as our Father that doeth all things well, our Father that ordereth all. Thus may we, knowing that all things are in Thy hands, abide Thy time, patiently doing the work Thou hast given us to do—Amen.

George Dawson.

September the Fourth

Grant, we beseech Thee, Almighty God, that as we are bathed in the new light of Thy everlasting truth, so our clear sight of Thee in heart and mind may become sincere obedience to Thee in word and deed—Amen.

Rowland Williams.

Almighty God, who art the Giver of all wisdom, enlighten my understanding with knowledge of right, and govern my will by Thy laws, that no deceit may mislead me, nor temptation corrupt me; that I may always endeavor to do good, and to hinder evil. Amidst all the hopes and fears of this world, take not Thy Holy Spirit from me; but grant that my thoughts may be fixed on Thee, and that I may finally attain everlasting happiness, for Jesus Christ's sake—Amen.

Samuel Johnson (1709-1784).

September the Fifth ✢ ✢ ✢ ✢ ✢ ✢ 249

Eternal God, who hast neither dawn nor evening, yet sendest us alternate mercies of the darkness and the day; there is no light but Thine, without, within. As Thou liftest the curtain of night from our abodes, take also the veil from all our hearts. Rise with Thy morning upon our souls: quicken all our labor and our prayer: and though all else declines, let the noontide of Thy grace and peace remain. May we walk, while it is yet day, in the steps of Him who, with fewest hours, finished Thy divinest work—Amen.

James Martineau.

Lord, make us to resemble even here the heavenly kingdom, through mutual love, where all hatred is quite banished, and all is full of love, and, consequently, full of joy and gladness—Amen.

Ludovicus Vives, 1578.

Eternal and most glorious God, suffer me not so to undervalue myself as to give away my soul, Thy soul, Thy dear and precious soul, for nothing; and all the world is nothing, if the soul must be given for it. Preserve therefore, my soul, O Lord, because it belongs to Thee, and preserve my body because it belongs to my soul. Thou alone dost steer my boat through all its voyage, but hast a more especial care of it, when it comes to a narrow current, or to a dangerous fall of waters. Thou hast a care of the preservation of my body in all the ways of my life; but, in the straits of death, open Thine eyes wider, and enlarge Thy Providence towards me so far that no illness or agony may shake and benumb the soul. Do Thou so make my bed in all my sickness that, being used to Thy hand, I may be content with any bed of Thy making—Amen.

John Donne (1573-1631).

Warm my cold heart, Lord, I beseech Thee. Take away all that hinders me from giving myself to Thee. Mould me according to Thine own image. Give me grace to obey Thee in all things, and ever to follow Thy gracious leading. Make me this day to be kind to my fellow-men, to be gentle and unselfish, careful to hurt no one by word or deed, but anxious to do good to all, and to make others happy. O Lord, forgive the sins of my temper. Pardon all my hasty words and unchristian thoughts. Make me watchful, that I offend not with my tongue. Give me a meek and loving spirit, which is in Thy sight of great price. I would not live unto myself, but unto Thee. Keep me from sin this day, and all that may offend Thee ; for Jesus Christ's sake—Amen.

Ashton Oxenden.

Good Lord, who alone orderest all things well, I cast myself wholly upon Thine infinite mercy; I trust Thee with my all, myself, and all whom I love, and all which I desire; my present and my future, my hopes and my fears, my time and my eternity, my joys and my sorrows. Deal with me as Thou willest, and knowest best, only bind me safe to Thine everlasting love—Amen.

Treasury of Devotion, 1869.

Lord, Thou Fountain of goodness, whose tender mercies are over all Thy works, and who hast compassion on them that fear Thee, even as a father pitieth his children; amid the many changes and sorrows of this earthly life, grant us a patient resignation to Thy will, and contentment under all the rulings of Thy Providence—Amen.

New Church Book of Worship, 1876.

September the Ninth ✧ ✧ ✧ ✧ ✧ 253

Lord, give us grace, we beseech Thee, to hear and obey Thy voice which saith to every one of us "This is the way, walk ye in it." Nevertheless, let us not hear it behind us saying, This is the way; but rather before us saying, Follow me. When Thou puttest us forth, go before us; when the way is too great for us, carry us; in the darkness of death, comfort us; in the day of resurrection, satisfy us— Amen.

Christina G. Rossetti.

Be Thou Thyself, O Lord, the Sanctifier and the Shepherd of Thy people, that we who are strengthened by Thy help, may, in our daily life, walk with Thee, and in all quietness of spirit serve Thee, through Jesus Christ our Master—Amen.

Roman Breviary.

Lord, I offer unto Thee all my sins and offences, which I have committed before Thee, from the day wherein I first could sin even to this hour; that Thou mayest consume and burn them, one and all, with the fire of Thy love, and do away all the stains of my sins, and cleanse my conscience from all offences, and restore to me Thy grace, fully forgiving me all, and admitting me mercifully to the kiss of peace. I offer up also unto Thee all that is good in me, though it be very small and imperfect, in order that Thou mayest amend and sanctify it, that Thou mayest make it grateful and acceptable unto Thee, and always be perfecting it more and more; and bring me also, slothful and unprofitable poor creature as I am, to a good and blessed end— Amen.

Thomas à Kempis.

September the Eleventh

Thou, O my God, art ever new, though Thou art the most ancient. Thou alone art the food for eternity. I am to live for ever; not for a time—and I have no power over my being; I must live on, with intellect and consciousness for ever, in spite of myself. Without Thee eternity would be another name for eternal misery. In Thee alone have I that which can stay me up for ever; Thou alone art the food of my soul. Thou alone art inexhaustible, and ever offerest to me something new to know, something new to love. And so on for eternity I shall ever be a little child beginning to be taught the rudiments of Thy infinite Divine nature. For Thou art Thyself the seat and centre of all good, and the only substance in this universe of shadows, and the heaven in which blessed spirits live and rejoice—Amen.

John Henry Newman.

O God, our true Life, in whom and by whom all things live, Thou commandest us to seek Thee, and art ready to be found; Thou biddest us knock, and openest when we do so. To know Thee is life, to serve Thee is freedom, to enjoy Thee is a kingdom, to praise Thee is the joy and happiness of the soul. I praise, and bless, and adore Thee, I worship Thee, I glorify Thee, I give thanks to Thee for Thy great glory. I humbly beseech Thee to abide with me, to reign in me, to make this heart of mine a holy temple, a fit habitation for Thy Divine majesty. O Thou Maker and Preserver of all things, visible and invisible! keep, I beseech Thee, the work of Thine own hands, who trusts in Thy mercy alone for safety and protection. Guard me with the power of Thy grace, here and in all places, now and at all times, forevermore—Amen.

St. Augustine (354–430).

September the Thirteenth +++ 257

O Thou, who hast taught us to seek first Thy kingdom and its righteousness, teach me to say, "Thy will be done" before I say, "give me my daily bread." Teach me to accept Thy will as the foundation of my happiness, and other things as only its superstructure. I am more afraid of the hunger of the body than of the hunger of the spirit. Convince me that it would not profit a man to gain the whole world, and lose his own soul. Show me that it is only the possession of my soul that makes the possession of the world any gain. Impress me with the truth that no *thing* can give me joy, if I myself am not already joyful. Inspire me with the knowledge that the issues of life are not from without but from within. Guide me into the discovery that the pleasures at Thy right hand are the only things that are "pleasures *for evermore*"—Amen.

George Matheson.

Remember, O most pitying Father, what this frail and feeble work of Thine hands can bear without fainting; nothing, indeed, of itself, but all things in Thee, if strengthened by Thy grace. Wherefore grant me strength, that I may suffer and endure; patience alone I ask. Lord, give me this, and behold my heart is ready. O God, my heart is ready to receive whatsoever shall be laid upon me. Grant that in my patience I may possess my soul; to that end, may I often look upon the face of Christ Thy Son, that, as He hath suffered such terrible things in the flesh, I may endeavor to be armed with the same mind. Wherefore I commit my strength unto Thee, O Lord; for Thou art my Strength and my Refuge. Keep me, and bring me safely out of this trial when it shall please Thee—Amen.

Treasury of Devotion, 1869.

September the Fifteenth ✤ ✤ ✤ ✤ 259

We give Thee thanks, Almighty God, for the bread of the body that perisheth, and we beseech Thee to give us that bread by which man's higher life is fed, that we, laying hold of the life that never dies, may thereby be fitted for the troubles and burdens of this life, and look forward with joy to the higher and better life. So may we live in constant childlike trust in Thee, as to believe, though we behold it not, that the end of all things is divine, and to catch the music to which this world is set by Thee. Lead Thou us from the lower life to the better life, that little things may lose their power to vex us, and in the midst of the troubles of this life, we may have the peace of God that passeth all understanding. Of Thy loving-kindness and tender mercy hear us, through Jesus Christ our Lord—Amen.

George Dawson.

God, in Thee alone can our wearied spirits find full satisfaction and rest, and in Thy love is the highest joy. Lord, if we have Thee we have enough; and we are happy if Thou wilt but give peace to our consciences, and make us know how gracious and merciful Thou art. Preserve in our hearts that peace which passeth all understanding; and make us better and holier in time to come. Strengthen those of us who are in any sorrow or perplexity by the inward comfort of Thy Holy Spirit, and bid us know that our light affliction, which is but for a moment, worketh for us a far more exceeding and eternal weight of glory. For there will come a time when Thou wilt bring us to the place of perfect rest, where we shall behold Thy face in righteousness, and be satisfied from Thy eternal fulness—Amen.

Melchior Ritter, 1689.

September the Seventeenth + + + 261

Dearest Lord, be not weary of my slothfulness in serving Thee, but help me by the indwelling of Thy Spirit, to struggle on through every hindrance to the perfect day, overcoming as Thou mayest see best every temptation which keeps me apart from Thee, and, in the end, giving me that blessed freedom which is the portion of Thy children, freedom from self and sin, and the enjoyment of that communion with Thee which is the end of all sanctification. Pour down, Lord, the fulness of Thy grace on all I love, shed abroad Thy love into the hearts of those dearest to me, and draw them near unto Thyself, that the full beauty and truth that is in Thee may be revealed to those who know Thee but in part. So shall Thy name be glorified and Thy love perfected in them, and Thy poor servant shall praise Thy mercy forever— Amen.

Maria Hare.

September the Eighteenth

Almighty God, who hast caused the light of eternal life to shine upon the world, we beseech Thee that our hearts may be so kindled with heavenly desires, and Thy love so shed abroad in us by Thy Holy Spirit, that we may continually seek the things which are above; and, abiding in purity of heart and mind, may at length attain unto Thine everlasting kingdom, there to dwell in the glorious light of Thy presence, world without end— Amen.

Book of Prayers, 1851.

O God, whose never-failing Providence ordereth all things both in heaven and earth; we humbly beseech Thee to put away from us all hurtful things, and to give us those things which are profitable for us, through Jesus Christ our Lord— Amen.

Gelasian, A. D. 492.

September the Nineteenth + + + 263

God, since Thou art Love, and he that loveth not Thee and his brethren knoweth Thee not, and abideth in death, deliver us from injustice, envy, hatred, and malice; give us grace to pardon all who have offended us, and to bear with one another, even as Thou, Lord, dost bear with us, in Thy patience and great loving-kindness—Amen.

Eugène Bersier, 1874.

God, who art the Author of love, and the Lover of pure peace and affection, let all who are terrified by fears, afflicted by poverty, harassed by tribulation, worn down by illness, be set free by Thine indulgent tenderness, raised up by amendment of life, and cherished by Thy daily compassion, through Jesus Christ our Lord—Amen.

Gallican Sacramentary, A. D. 800.

September the Twentieth

We beseech Thee, O Lord, remember all for good; have mercy upon all, O God. Remember every soul who, being in any affliction, trouble, or agony, stands in need of Thy mercy and help, all who are in necessity or distress; all who love, or hate us.

Thou, O Lord, art the Helper of the helpless; the Hope of the hopeless; the Saviour of them who are tossed with tempests; the Haven of them who sail; be Thou All to all. The glorious majesty of the Lord our God be upon us; prosper Thou the work of our hands upon us; Oh, prosper Thou our handy-work. Lord, be Thou within me, to strengthen me; without me, to keep me; above me, to protect me; beneath me, to uphold me; before me, to direct me; behind me, to keep me from straying; round about me, to defend me. Blessed be Thou O Lord, our Father, for ever and ever—Amen.

Lancelot Andrewes (1555-1626).

September the Twenty-first + + 265

When we are awake, we are still with Thee, O God most merciful, and Thy hand is over us for good. Be Thou the Desire of our hearts, and the Ruler of our thoughts. O heavenly Father, we need Thy love and Thy calm breath shed abroad in our souls to be a fountain of strength; we know not without Thee what may befall us this day, either of peril, or of temptation, or of sorrow. But Thou canst put a guard about our path, and canst fence all our senses from temptation by sobering them with Thy holy fear. Give us, then, we pray Thee, a right sense of duty, to shield us in all conflict, and guard us against sin and death. Lead us not into temptation; or, when we are tempted, deliver us by humble watchfulness from all power of evil—Amen.

Rowland Williams.

September the Twenty-second

We beseech Thee, O Lord, that Thou wouldest keep our tongues from evil, and our lips from speaking guile; that, as Thy holy angels ever sing Thy praises in heaven, so with our tongues may we at all times glorify Thee on earth—Amen.

Roman Breviary.

Into the hands of Thy blessed protection and unspeakable mercy, O Lord, I commend this day my soul and my body, with all the faculties, powers, and actions of them both; beseeching Thee to be ever with me, to direct, sanctify, and govern me in the ways of Thy laws, and in the works of Thy commandments; that, through Thy most mighty protection, both here and ever, I may be preserved in body and soul, to serve Thee the only true God, through Jesus Christ our Lord—Amen.

Private Devotions, 1560.

September the Twenty-third ✠ ✠ 267

   Lord, of Thy tender love, prepare Thou Thyself a place for Thyself in my heart. Empty my heart of every feeling, thought, emotion, desire, purpose, anxiety, hope, fear, which may interfere with Thy love. Open my whole heart to receive Thee; let nothing shut Thee out, nothing be shut to Thee. Thou alone canst fit my heart for Thyself; cleanse it wholly by Thy Spirit, that it may wholly love Thee; be wholly filled with Thee; wholly penetrated, enlightened, warmed, by Thee; that Thou mayest dwell in it forever, and it may love Thee with Thine own love in it everlastingly—Amen.

E. B. Pusey.

ook upon me, O Lord, and pity me; make me, and let me be Thine by the choice of my will—Amen.

Thomas Wilson (1663-1755).

September the Twenty-fourth

In confidence of Thy goodness and great mercy, O Lord, I draw near unto Thee, as a sick person to the Healer, as one hungry and thirsty to the Fountain of life, a creature to the Creator, a desolate soul to my own tender Comforter. Behold, in Thee is all whatsoever I can or ought to desire; Thou art my Salvation and my Redemption, my Hope and my Strength. Rejoice therefore this day the soul of Thy servant; for unto Thee, O Lord, have I lifted up my soul—Amen.

Thomas à Kempis.

O Lord, who dost wash out our offences, do Thou comfort us who faithfully call upon Thee; and, we beseech Thee, that Thou wouldest blot out our transgressions, and restore us from death to the land of the living, through Christ our Lord—Amen.

Sarum Breviary, A. D. 1085.

September the Twenty-fifth ✦ ✦ 269

God, who of Thy great love to this world, didst reconcile earth to heaven through Thine Only-begotten Son; grant that we who, by the darkness of our sins, are turned aside from brotherly love, may by Thy light shed forth in our souls be filled with Thine own sweetness, and embrace our friends in Thee, and our enemies for Thy sake, in a bond of mutual affection—Amen.

Mozarabic before A. D. 700.

Lord, strengthen and support, I entreat Thee, all persons unjustly accused or underrated. Comfort them by the ever-present thought that Thou knowest the whole truth, and wilt in Thine own good time make their righteousness as clear as the light. Give them grace to pray for such as do them wrong, and hear and bless them when they pray—Amen.

Christina G. Rossetti.

270 ✤ ✤ September the Twenty-sixth

O Lord, fix my soul on Thee; let me not weary myself with cares and anxieties and harass of this life, who hope to live with Thee in Thine everlasting love. Let me not be anxious about anything, save that Thou shouldest love me, and make my soul as Thou lovest and willest—Amen.

E. B. Pusey.

Be Thou, O God, a Refuge from the storm, and a Shadow from the heat. Even whilst we are lying safely in Thine arms, we are sometimes foolishly timid. Oh, help our unbelief, and, in Thy tenderness, assure us of Thy protection. Thou canst make all things work together for good to them that love Thee. Let not calamity injure our souls; let not sorrow corrode our hearts—Amen.

Hunter's Devotional Services, 1892.

September the Twenty-seventh

Almighty God, who art the Strength of all who put their trust in Thee, grant unto us in the midst of the troubles of this mortal life, that, being confident in Thy wisdom and goodness, and Thine abiding love, we may endure all things in a quiet spirit, seeking ever in the midst of the things of this world to meditate ofttimes upon the divine peace, and the heavenly rest of the glorified spirits of light ; and being held up by Thy mercy, may neither faint nor fear, but pass on, doing faithfully the duties of life, and, in our last hour, supporting by the Everlasting arms, we beseech Thee to guide us into the life everlasting. This we do ask, in the name of Jesus Christ Our Lord —Amen.

George Dawson.

Searcher of all hearts, Thou knowest my heart, and how it stands with me. Thou hast made it, Thou knowest whether I love Thee. All I am or have that has any goodness in it, I am or have alone through Thee, for it is all Thy work in me ; but it must be Thine also by the free surrender of my heart. In Thy service, and fulfilling Thy will, I would fain spend every minute of my life. The thought of Thee shall be the sweetest to me of all thoughts ; to speak of Thee the dearest and best of all I speak or hear ; the joy of Thy love shall be the inmost joy of my soul. Gladly would I devote my whole being to Thee ; accept me, then, as a living sacrifice, and give me the mind that was in Christ Jesus, to the glory of God the Father—Amen.

Michael Sailer (1751-1832).

September the Twenty-ninth ✧ ✧ 273

Holy Father, whose chosen way of manifesting Thyself to Thy children is by the discipline of trial and pain, we rejoice that we can turn to Thee in the midst of great anxiety, and commit all our troubles to Thy sure help. As Thou art with us in the sunlight, Oh, be Thou with us in the cloud. In the path by which Thou guidest us, though it be through desert and stormy sea, suffer not our faith to fail, but sustain us by Thy near presence, and let the comforts which are in Jesus Christ fill our hearts with peace. And, O God, grant that the fiery trial which trieth us may not be in vain, but may lead us to a cheerful courage, and a holy patience; and let patience have her perfect work, that we may be perfect and entire, wanting nothing, wholly consecrate to Thee, through Jesus Christ our Lord—Amen.

Henry W. Foote.

O Eternal God, who hast created me to do the work of God after the manner of men, and to serve Thee in this generation, and according to my capacities; give me Thy grace that I may be a prudent spender of my time, so as I may best prevent or resist all temptation, and be profitable to the Christian commonwealth; and, by discharging all my duty, may glorify Thy name. Take from me all slothfulness, and give me a diligent and an active spirit, and wisdom to choose my employment; that I may do works proportionable to my person, and to the dignity of a Christian, and may fill up all the spaces of my time with actions of religion and charity; improving my talent intrusted to me by Thee, my Lord, that I may enter into the joy of the Lord, to partake of Thy eternal felicities, even for Thy mercy's sake—Amen.

Jeremy Taylor (1613-1667).

October the First ✢ ✢ ✢ ✢ ✢ ✢ ✢ 275

 God, who leadest us through seasons of life to be partakers of Thine eternity; the shadows of our evening hasten on. Quicken us betimes: and spare us that sad word, "The harvest is past, the summer is ended, and we are not saved." Anew we dedicate ourselves to Thee. We would ask nothing, reserve nothing, for ourselves, save only leave to go whither Thou mayest guide, to live not far from Thee, and die into Thy nearer light. Content to accept the reproach of truth, we would take upon us the yoke of Christ, whom it behooved to suffer ere He entered into His glory—Amen.

James Martineau.

Bless us, O Lord, with Thy heavenly benediction; so that, rejoicing in Thy strength, and trusting in Thy loving-kindness, we may obtain a blessed immortality—Amen.

Sarum Breviary, A. D. 1085.

Thou art the Comfort of all who trust Thee, the Help and Shield of all who hope in Thee. O Lord my God, from Thy hand I accept all things without a murmur, for whatever Thou dost is right. Is it Thy will that I walk in darkness? Behold, Thy way is good, and I will praise Thee. Wilt Thou that my path be light and peace? Again I praise Thee; Thy grace orders all things, and at all times. One thing only be far from me: I entreat Thee, let me not walk in sin and unrighteousness, nor be counted among them who care not for Thee. Let my will be only Thine, then I shall fear nothing, no suffering and no death, and all things must work together for my good. Lord, keep me in Thy love and truth, comfort me with Thy light, and guide me by Thy Spirit—Amen.

S. Weiss (1738–1805).

October the Third — 277

Our Father, grant us, this day, the sense of Thy presence to cheer, and Thy light to direct us, and give us strength for Thy service. And yet more, Father, give us Thine own help and blessing in our sorrows, our faintness, our failure and sin. Thou knowest that we cannot bear our burdens alone. We are only little children, and the world seems very dark to us, and our path very hard, if we are alone. But we are Thy little children; and so we know we can come to our Father, to ask Thee to help us, and enliven us, and strengthen us, and give us hope. We are not ashamed of our tears, for our Lord has wept with us. We do not ask Thee to take away our sorrow, for He was made perfect through suffering; but we do ask Thee to be with us as Thou wert with Him, our Father, close to Thy little ones, even as He has promised us —Amen.

The Altar at Home, 1862.

Blessed are all Thy saints, my God and King, who have travelled over the tempestuous sea of mortality, and have at last made the desired port of peace and felicity. Oh, cast a gracious eye upon us who are still in our dangerous voyage. Remember and succor us in our distress, and think on them that lie exposed to the rough storms of troubles and temptations. Strengthen our weakness, that we may do valiantly in this spiritual war; help us against our own negligence and cowardice, and defend us from the treachery of our unfaithful hearts. We are exceeding frail, and indisposed to every virtuous and gallant undertaking. Grant, O Lord, that we may bring our vessel safe to shore, unto our desired haven—Amen.

St. Augustine (354–430).

October the Fifth ✠ ✠ ✠ ✠ ✠ ✠ ✠

Lord, I know not what is before me this day, but Thou knowest. I desire to leave all in Thy hands, and to place myself at Thy disposal. Do for me as Thou seest best. Prosper me in all that I undertake. Give me good success, if it be Thy will. But, if Thou seest that crosses and disappointments are better for me, give me grace to accept them as from Thee. Enable me to bear them meekly and cheerfully, and to say, Father, not my will, but Thine, be done. O my God, make me happy this day in Thy service. Keep my conscience void of offence. Let me do nothing, say nothing, desire nothing, which is contrary to Thy will. Give me a thankful spirit. O for a heart to praise Thee for all that Thou hast given me, and for all Thou hast withheld from me —Amen.

Ashton Oxenden.

Thou Brightness of eternal glory, Thou Comfort of the pilgrim soul, with Thee is my tongue without voice, and my very silence speaketh unto Thee. Come, Oh, come; for without Thee I shall have no joyful day or hour; for Thou art my joy, and without Thee my table is empty. Praise and glory be unto Thee; let my mouth, my soul, and all creatures together, praise and bless Thee—Amen.

Thomas à Kempis.

Thou, **who art the eternal protec-**tion and salvation of our souls, arm us, we entreat Thee, with the helmet of hope, and the shield of Thy invincible defence; that so, helped by Thee in the straits of our necessities, we may be filled with joy and gladness with those who love Thee, through Jesus Christ our Lord—Amen.

Sarum Breviary, A. D. 1085.

October the Seventh + + + + + + 281

**I** Thank Thee, O my God, that Thou hast made me, redeemed me, and hast kept me in Thy grace until now. Thy mercy is it, O my God, if I have done any good, or that I have been kept from any evil. Blessed be Thou for every good thought Thou hast put into my heart, and for the grace to obey it; for every blessing without and within. With my whole soul, and all its powers, and above its powers, I would praise Thee. Lord, help me Thyself to praise Thee, with the silent praise of thankful love—Amen.

E. B. Pusey.

Open wide the window of our spirits, and fill us full of light; open wide the door of our hearts, that we may receive and entertain Thee with all our powers of adoration and love—Amen.

Christina G. Rossetti.

October the Eighth

Lord, lift up the light of Thy countenance upon us: let Thy peace rule in our hearts; and may it be our strength and our song, in the house of our pilgrimage. We commit ourselves to Thy care and keeping this day; let Thy grace be mighty in us, and sufficient for us, and let it work in us both to will and to do of Thine own good pleasure, and grant us strength for all the duties of the day. Keep us from sin; give us the rule over our own spirits; and keep us from speaking unadvisedly with our lips. May we live together in peace and holy love, and do Thou command Thy blessing upon us, even life for evermore. Prepare us for all the events of the day; for we know not what a day may bring forth. Give us grace to deny ourselves; to take up our cross daily, and to follow in the steps of our Lord and Master—Amen.

Matthew Henry (1662-1714).

October the Ninth ✦ ✦ ✦ ✦ ✦ ✦ ✦ 283

Almighty God, we bless and praise Thee that we have wakened to the light of another earthly day; and now we will think of what a day should be. Our days are Thine, let them be spent for Thee. Our days are few, let them be spent with care. There are dark days behind us, forgive their sinfulness; there may be dark days before us, strengthen us for their trials. We pray Thee to shine on this day—the day which we may call our own. Lord, we go to our daily work; help us to take pleasure therein. Show us clearly what our duty is; help us to be faithful in doing it. Let all we do be well done, fit for Thine eye to see. Give us strength to do, patience to bear; let our courage never fail. When we cannot love our work, let us think of it as Thy task; and, by our true love to Thee, make unlovely things shine in the light of Thy great love—Amen.

George Dawson.

October the Tenth

Grant, we beseech Thee, merciful Lord, to thy faithful people pardon and peace, that they may be cleansed from all their sins, and serve Thee with a quiet mind; through Jesus Christ our Lord—Amen.

Gelasian, A. D. 492.

O God, whose eternal Providence has embarked our souls in the ship of our bodies, not to expect any port of anchorage on the sea of this world, but to steer through it to Thy glorious kingdom, preserve us, O Lord, from the dangers that on all sides assault us, and keep our affections still fitly disposed to receive Thy holy inspirations; that, being carried sweetly and strongly forward by Thy Holy Spirit, we may happily arrive at last in the haven where we would be; through Jesus Christ our Lord—Amen.

Wickes' Devotions, 1700.

October the Eleventh ✢ ✢ ✢ ✢ ✢ 285

O God, from whom we have received life and all earthly blessings, vouchsafe to give unto us each day what we need; give unto all of us strength to perform faithfully our appointed tasks, bless the work of our hands and of our minds. Grant that we may ever serve Thee, in sickness and in health, in necessity and in abundance, sanctify our joys and our trials; and give us grace to seek first Thy kingdom and its righteousness, in the sure and certain faith that all else shall be added unto us—Amen.

Eugène Bersier.

O God, who art Love, grant to Thy children to bear one another's burdens in perfect goodwill, that Thy peace which passeth understanding may keep our hearts and minds in Christ Jesus our Lord—Amen.

Book of Hours, 1865.

Soften our hearts, O Lord, that we may be moved no less at the necessities and griefs of our neighbors, than if they concerned ourselves, or the cases that touched us nearest, and let us think them to befall even to our dearest friends. Let us pity them as ourselves, and, in their adversity, let us have compassion upon them, that, as we would have pitied ourselves for the like cause, so we may be moved with pity towards those, whom we see oppressed with the same adversities—Amen.

Ludovicus Dives, 1578.

Confirm, O Lord, we pray Thee, the hearts of Thy children, and strengthen them with the power of Thy grace; that they may both be devout in prayer to Thee, and sincere in love for each other; through Jesus Christ our Lord—Amen.

Leonine, A. D. 440.

October the Thirteenth ✧ ✧ ✧ ✧ ✧ 287

**O Lord, our heavenly Father,** Almighty and everlasting God, who hast safely brought us to the beginning of this day, defend us in the same with Thy mighty power; and grant that this day we fall into no sin, neither run into any kind of danger; but that all our doings, being ordered by Thy governance, may be righteous in Thy sight; through Jesus Christ our Lord—Amen.

Gelasian Sacramentary, A.D. 494.

O Lord, who hast mercy upon all, take away from me my sins, and mercifully kindle in me the fire of Thy Holy Spirit. Take away from me the heart of stone, and give me a heart of flesh, a heart to love and adore Thee, a heart to delight in Thee, to follow and to enjoy Thee, for Christ's sake—Amen.

St. Ambrose (340–397).

Oh, teach us to know Thee, our God, and enable us to do Thy will as we ought to do. Give us hearts to love Thee, to trust and delight in Thee, and to adhere and cleave in faithfulness unto Thee. That no temptations may draw us, nor any tribulations drive us, from Thee; but that all Thy dispensations to us, and all Thy dealings with us, may be the messengers of Thy love to our souls, to bring us still nearer to Thy blessed self, and to make us still fitter for Thy heavenly kingdom —Amen.

Benjamin Jenks (1646–1724).

Lord, we beseech Thee mercifully to hear our prayers, and stretch forth the right hand of Thy power against all things that fight against us; through Jesus Christ our Lord—Amen.

Roman Breviary.

October the Fifteenth — 289

**Lord, in whom is the Truth,** help us, we entreat Thee, to speak the truth in love, to hate a lie, to eschew exaggeration, inaccuracy, affectation. Yea, though tribulation or persecution should arise for the Truth's sake, suffer us not to be offended—Amen.

Christina G. Rossetti.

Almighty Lord, and everlasting God, vouchsafe, we beseech Thee, to direct, sanctify, and govern, both our hearts and bodies, in the ways of Thy laws, and in the works of Thy commandments; that, through Thy most mighty protection, both here and ever, we may be preserved in body and soul; through our Lord and Saviour Jesus Christ—Amen.

Gregorian, A. D. 590.

Glory be to Thee, O Lord; glory be to Thee. That this day, and every day, may come on, perfect, holy, peaceable, healthful, and without sin,—grant, Lord, we beseech Thee. What things are good and profitable to our souls, together with peace in this world, grant, Lord, we beseech Thee. That we may accomplish the rest of our life, in repentance and godly fear, in health and peace, grant, Lord, we beseech Thee. Whatsoever things are true, whatsoever things are honest, whatsoever things are just, whatsoever things are pure, whatsoever things are of good report,—that we may think on these things to do them, grant, Lord, we beseech Thee. A Christian end of our life, without sin, without shame, and, if Thou thinkest good, without pain; when Thou wilt, and as Thou wilt, grant, Lord, we beseech Thee—Amen.

Lancelot Andrewes (1555-1626).

October the Seventeenth ✢ ✢ ✢ ✢ 291

Thou Hope of all holy and humble men of heart, and the Saviour of them that trust in Thee in time of trouble, give us not over as captives, in spiritual chains; but recover us, that we may awake to do Thy will. Lord, Thou knowest all our desire, and our secret sighing is not hidden from Thee. Into Thy hands I commend my soul and my prayer: give what Thou seest fit, and fit us for what Thou givest. Give us wisdom to abound, or patience to suffer need; and where the Master placed us, there to be content. Let all our work be done well before we come to die; and let us be gathered into Thine arms, as the harvesters gather a shock in full season. Let our death be happy; and our happiness beyond the power of death—Amen.

Rowland Williams.

October the Eighteenth

 Lord God, Holy Father, be Thou blessed both now and for evermore, because as Thou wilt, so is it done, and what Thou doest is good. My soul is sorrowful, sometimes, even unto tears; sometimes also my spirit is disquieted, by reason of impending sufferings. I long after the joy of Thy peace, the peace of Thy children I earnestly crave. If Thou give peace, if Thou pour into me holy joy, the soul of Thy servant shall be full of melody, and shall become devout in Thy praise. Make me a dutiful and humble disciple (as Thou art wont to be kind), that I may be ever ready to go, if Thou dost but beckon to me. Thou knowest what is expedient for my spiritual progress, and how greatly tribulation serves to scour off the rust of sins; do with me according to Thy desired good pleasure —Amen.

Thomas à Kempis.

Grant unto us, Almighty God, that when our vision fails, and our understanding is darkened; when the ways of life seem hard, and the brightness of life is gone,—to us grant the wisdom that deepens faith when the sight is dim, and enlarges trust when the understanding is not clear. And whensoever Thy ways in nature or in the soul are hard to be understood, then may our quiet confidence, our patient trust, our loving faith in Thee be great, and as children knowing that they are loved, cared for, guarded, kept, may we with a quiet mind at all times put our trust in the unseen God. So may we face life without fear, and death without fainting; and, whatsoever may be in the life to come, give us confident hope that whatsoever is best for us both here and hereafter is Thy good pleasure, and will be Thy law—Amen.

George Dawson.

**Lord God, Father of mercies,** the Fountain of comfort and blessing, of life and peace, of plenty and pardon, who fillest heaven with Thy glory, and earth with Thy goodness; I give Thee the most earnest, and most humble returns of my glad and thankful heart, for Thou hast refreshed me with Thy comforts, and enlarged me with Thy blessing; for, besides the blessings of all mankind, the blessings of nature and the blessings of grace, the support of every minute, and the comforts of every day, Thou hast poured out an excellent expression of Thy loving-kindness upon me. Thou, Lord, hast made me glad through Thy works; I will rejoice in giving praise for the operations of Thy hands. Blessed be the Lord which only doeth wondrous and gracious things. And blessed be the Name of His Majesty for ever; and all the earth shall be filled with His Majesty—Amen.

Jeremy Taylor (1613–1667).

October the Twenty-first ✦ ✦ ✦ ✦ 295

Almighty God! our heavenly Father, who hast given us in Thy Son Jesus Christ a fountain of life, which, springing up within us, can make all things new, we thank Thee for the deeper meaning which He gives to life,—for the quickened sense of duty, the faith under sorrow, the immortal hopes, which we owe to Him. And we pray that His divine instructions may be so received by us with grateful hearts, that no resistance of ours may hinder His freely working within us a miracle as when He changed the water into wine. In the power of His Spirit, may our griefs be transformed into consolations,—our infirmities into strength to do well,—our sins into repentance,—our fainting and halting spirits into an heavenly mind; and, finally, the doubts, the discouragements, the trials, of this earthly life, into the full assurance and unclouded bliss of an eternal life with Thee, through the same Jesus Christ our Lord—Amen.

Henry W. Foote.

October the Twenty-second

O God, the Father of our Lord Jesus Christ, our only Saviour, the Prince of Peace; give us grace seriously to lay to heart the great dangers we are in by our unhappy divisions. Take away from us all hatred and prejudice, and whatsoever else may hinder us from godly union and concord; that as there is but one body, and one Spirit, and one hope of our calling, one Lord, one faith, one baptism, one God and Father of us all, so we may henceforth be all of one heart, and of one soul, united in one holy bond of truth and peace, of faith and charity, and may with one mind and one mouth glorify Thee; through Jesus Christ our Lord—Amen.

Book of Common Prayer, A. D. 1626.

Thou knowest, O Lord, what most I require; help me, and out of the treasury of Thy goodness, succor Thou my needy soul—Amen. *E. B. Pusey.*

October the Twenty-third ✣ ✣ ✣ ✣ 297

God, who makest all things work together for good to them that love Thee, pour into our hearts such steadfast love to Thee, that those desires which spring from Thee may not be turned aside by any temptation—Amen.

Roman Breviary.

Pour into our hearts the spirit of unselfishness, so that, when our cup overflows, we may seek to share our happiness with our brethren. O Thou God of Love, who makest Thy sun to rise on the evil and on the good, and sendest rain on the just and the unjust, grant that we may become more and more Thy true children, by receiving into our souls more of Thine own spirit of ungrudging and unwearying kindness; which we ask in the name of Jesus Christ—Amen.

Hunter's Devotional Services, 1892.

My God, possess my soul with such an ardent love of Thee, so buoyant above all other affections, that no one may ever come in competition with it; such a love as may not only subdue all other affections, but purify and make them innocent; such a love as may create in my soul a perpetual pleasure in the contemplation of Thee, and a continual thirst after Thee; a love which may transport my soul with Thy divine perfections, and paint there such bright ideas of Thy glorious majesty, that none of the trifling pleasures and temptations of this world may be able to make on it the least impression. And as, my gracious Lord, Thou hast given me much, and forgiven me much, so raise my love to a degree proportionable to Thy bounty and mercy—Amen.

Charles How (1661-1745).

Lord God, our Governor, we beseech Thee, of Thy mercy, that we may have the heavenly vision, and behold things as they seem unto Thee, that the turmoil of this world may be seen by us to be bringing forth the sweet peace of the eternal years, and that in all the troubles and sorrows of our own hearts we may behold good, and so, with quiet mind and inward peace, careless of outward storm, we may do the duty of life which brings to us a quiet heart, ever trusting in Thee. We give Thee thanks for all Thy mercy. We beseech Thy forgiveness of all our sins. We pray Thy guidance in all things, Thy presence in the hour of death, Thy glory in the life to come. Of Thy mercy hear us, through Jesus Christ our Lord—Amen.

George Dawson.

October the Twenty-sixth

Almighty and everlasting God, preserve the works of Thy mercy, and pour into our hearts the sweetness of Thy most holy love, and of entire devotion to Thy holy will—Amen.

Rowland Williams.

O Lord who hearest prayer, give ear unto our petitions; that we who, taken captive by our sins, are as it were withered like grass, may be delivered by Thy divine mercy—Amen.

Sarum Breviary, A. D. 1085.

O Lord from whom all good things do come, grant to us, Thy humble servants, that by Thy holy inspiration we may think those things that are good, and by Thy merciful guiding may perform the same, through our Lord Jesus Christ—Amen.

Gelasian, A. D. 492.

October the Twenty-seventh ✢ ✢ 301

May my whole being, O God, be one thanksgiving unto Thee, may all within me praise Thee and love Thee; for all which Thou hast forgiven, and for all which Thou hast given; for Thine unknown hidden blessings, and for those which, in my negligence or thoughtlessness, I passed over; for any and every gift of nature or of grace; for my power of loving; for all blessings within and without; and for all which Thou hast yet in store for me; for everything whereby Thou hast drawn me to Thyself, whether joy or sorrow; for all whereby Thou willest to make me Thine own for ever —Amen.

E. B. Pusey.

I Will whatsoever Thou willest; I will because Thou willest; I will in that manner Thou willest; I will as long as Thou willest—Amen.

Treasury of Devotion, 1869.

October the Twenty-eighth

O Lord God, in whose hand are the wills and affections of men, kindle in my mind holy desires, and repress sinful and corrupt imaginations; enable me to love Thy commandments, and to desire Thy promises; let me, by Thy protection and influence, so pass through things temporal, as finally not to lose the things eternal; and, among the hopes and fears, the pleasures and sorrows, the dangers and deliverances, and all the changes of this life, let my heart be surely fixed, by the help of Thy Holy Spirit, on the everlasting fruition of Thy presence, where true joys are to be found. Grant, O Lord, these petitions. Forgive, O merciful Lord, whatever I have done contrary to Thy laws, for Jesus Christ's sake—Amen.

Samuel Johnson (1709-1784).

October the Twenty-ninth ✢ ✢ ✢ 303

O God, our everlasting Hope! as disciples of One who had not where to lay His head, may we freely welcome the toils and sufferings of our humanity, and seek only strength to glorify the cross Thou layest on us. Every work of our hand may we do unto Thee; in every trouble, trace some lights of Thine; and let no blessing fall on dry and thankless hearts. Redeeming the time, may we fill every waking hour with faithful duty and well-ordered affections, as the sacrifice which Thou hast provided. Fill us with patient tenderness for others, seeing that we also are in the same case before Thee; and make us ready to help, and quick to forgive. And then, fix every grace, compose every fear, by a steady trust in Thine eternal realities—Amen.

James Martineau.

304 ✠ ✠ ✠ ✠ ✠ October the Thirtieth

O Lord, let that become possible to me by Thy grace, which by nature seems impossible to me. Thou knowest that I am able to suffer but little, and that I am quickly cast down, when a slight adversity ariseth. For Thy Name's sake, let every exercise of tribulation be amiable and desirable to me; for to suffer and to be disquieted for Thy sake is very wholesome for my soul—Amen.

Thomas à Kempis.

Almighty and everlasting God, who, in the abundance of Thy goodness, dost exceed the deserts as well as the desires of Thy suppliants, pour forth upon us Thy mercy; that Thou mayest forgive those things whereof our conscience is afraid, and add unto us those things which our prayer dareth not to ask; through Jesus Christ our Lord—Amen.

Gelasian, A. D. 492.
Sarum Breviary, A. D. 1085.

October the Thirty-first ✦ ✦ ✦ ✦ 305

 God, the Father of Consolation, let me neither desire anything against Thy will, nor in disappointment seek comfort away from Thee; but, knowing Thy will to comprehend what is best, in both my own life and my neighbor's, and in that of all creatures, let me ever resign myself to Thy disposal, who out of evil bringest good, and to whom our prayer should be in perfect peace. Give us what Thou seest fit, only fit us for what Thou givest—Amen.

       Rowland Williams.

O Lord, who dost promise a crown of life to them that love Thee, give us grace to love Thee for what Thou art more than for all which Thou bestowest; and so loving Thee, to endure temptation and finish our course with joy—Amen.

      Christina G. Rossetti.

November the First

Almighty God, we do offer unto Thee most high praise, and hearty thanks for all Thy wonderful graces and virtues which Thou hast manifested in all Thy saints, and in all other holy persons upon earth, who by their lives and labors have shined forth as lights in the several generations of the world; such as were the holy prophets, apostles, and martyrs, whom we remember with honor, and commemorate with joy; and for whom, as also for all other Thy happy servants, our fathers and brethren, who have departed this life with the seal of faith, we praise and magnify Thy holy Name; most humbly desiring that we may still continue in their holy communion, and enjoy the comfort thereof, following, with a glad will and mind, their holy examples of godly living, and steadfastness in Thy faith—Amen.

Private Devotions, 1560.

We thank Thee for the dear and faithful dead, for those who have made the distant heavens a Home for us, and whose truth and beauty are even now in our hearts. One by one Thou dost gather the scattered families out of the earthly light into the heavenly glory, from the distractions and strife and weariness of time to the peace of eternity. We thank Thee for the labors and the joys of these mortal years. We thank Thee for our deep sense of the mysteries that lie beyond our dust, and for the eye of faith which Thou hast opened for all who believe in Thy Son to outlook that mark. May we live altogether in Thy Faith and Love, and in that Hope which is full of Immortality—Amen.

Rufus Ellis.

O Lord, my God, Thou art to me whatsoever is good. Remember me because I am nothing, I have nothing, and I can do nothing. Thou alone art good, just, and holy; Thou canst do all things, Thou accomplishest all things, Thou fillest all things. Remember Thy mercies, and fill my heart with Thy grace, Thou who wilt not that Thy works should be void and in vain. Turn not Thy face away from me; withdraw not Thy consolation, lest my soul become as a thirsty land to Thee. Teach me, O Lord, to do Thy will; teach me to live worthily and humbly in Thy sight—Amen.

Thomas à Kempis.

Hear us, O Lord, we beseech Thee, and in our tribulations pity us, grant unto us spiritual gladness, and give us everlasting peace; through Christ our Lord—Amen.

Sarum Breviary, A. D. 1085.

November the Fourth ✦ ✦ ✦ ✦ ✦ 309

We yield Thee hearty thanks, O Lord our God, for Thy great goodness to us. Mercifully assist us in every duty each one of us has to do, and vouchsafe to be our Companion every day, from morning to night and night to morning; that we may love Thy presence and walk in it vigilantly, and, being delivered from all errors and adversities, may joyfully serve Thee in all godly quietness; and grant us Thy peace all the days of our life, through Jesus Christ our Lord—Amen.
James Skinner (1818-1882).

O Gracious Lord God, who deignest to make of man Thy mirror, that we in one another may behold Thine Image and love Thyself; unto every one of us grant, we beseech Thee, thus to love and thus to be beloved. For Jesus Christ's sake—Amen.
Christina G. Rossetti.

Eternal God, sanctify my body and soul, my thoughts and my intentions, my words and actions, that whatsoever I shall think, or speak, or do, may be by me designed for the glorification of Thy Name, and, by Thy blessing, it may be effective and successful in the work of God, according as it can be capable. Lord, turn my necessities into virtue; the works of nature into the works of grace; by making them orderly, regular, temperate; and let no pride or self-seeking, no covetousness or revenge, no little ends and low imaginations, pollute my spirit, and unhallow any of my words and actions; but let my body be a servant of my spirit, and both body and spirit servants of Jesus; that, doing all things for Thy glory here, I may be partaker of Thy glory hereafter, through Jesus Christ our Lord—Amen.

Jeremy Taylor (1613-1667).

November the Sixth ✦ ✦ ✦ ✦ ✦ ✦ 311

O God, our heavenly Father, we Thy children come now to Thy feet with our supplications. We cannot live without Thy blessing. Life is too hard for us and duty is too large. We get discouraged, and our feeble hands hang down. We come to Thee with our weakness, asking Thee for strength. Help us always to be of good cheer. Let us not be disheartened by difficulties. Let us never doubt Thy love or any of Thy promises. Give us grace to be encouragers of others, never discouragers. Let us not go about with sadness or fear among men, but may we be a benediction to every one we meet, always making life easier, never harder, for those who come within our influence. Help us to be as Christ to others, that they may see something of His love in our lives and learn to love Him in us. We beseech Thee to hear us, to receive our prayer, and to forgive our sins, for Jesus Christ's sake—Amen.

J. R. Miller.

November the Seventh

Look upon us, O Lord, and let all the darkness of our souls vanish before the beams of Thy brightness. Fill us with holy love, and open to us the treasures of Thy wisdom. All our desire is known unto Thee, therefore perfect what Thou hast begun, and what Thy Spirit has awakened us to ask in prayer. We seek Thy face, turn Thy face unto us and show us Thy glory. Then shall our longing be satisfied, and our peace shall be perfect —Amen.

St. Augustine (354-430).

O Lord, we beseech Thee mercifully to receive the prayers of Thy people who call upon Thee; and grant that they may both perceive and know what things they ought to do, and also may have grace and power faithfully to fulfil the same; through Jesus Christ our Lord—Amen.

Gregorian, A. D. 590.

November the Eighth ✦ ✦ ✦ ✦ ✦ 313

My God, I heartily thank Thee for all Thy goodness to my body and my soul. I want Thy guidance and direction in all I do. Let Thy wisdom counsel me, Thy hand lead me, and Thine arm support me. I put myself into Thy hands. Breathe into my soul holy and heavenly desires. Conform me to Thine own image. Make me like my Saviour. Enable me in some measure to live here on earth as He lived, and to act in all things as He would have acted—Amen.

Ashton Oxenden.

Living or dying, Lord, I would be Thine; keep me Thine own for ever, and draw me day by day nearer to Thyself, until I be wholly filled with Thy love, and fitted to behold Thee, face to face—Amen.

E. B. Pusey.

314 ✢ ✢ ✢ ✢ ✢ ✢ November the Ninth

Not only lay Thy commands on us, O Lord, but be pleased to enable us for the performance of every duty required of us. And so engage our hearts to Thyself, that we may make it our meat and drink to do Thy will, and, with enlarged hearts, run the way of Thy commands. Be merciful to us, and bless us, and keep us this day in all our ways. Let Thy love abound in our hearts, and sweetly and powerfully constrain us to all faithful and cheerful obedience—Amen.

Benjamin Jenks (1646-1724).

Almighty and everlasting God, who dost govern all things in heaven and earth, mercifully hear the supplications of Thy people, and grant us Thy peace all the days of our life; through Jesus Christ our Lord—Amen.

Gregorian, A. D. 590.

November the Tenth ✦ ✦ ✦ ✦ ✦ 315

My God, by whose loving Providence, sorrows, difficulties, trials, dangers, become means of grace, lessons of patience, channels of hope, grant us good will to use and not abuse those our privileges; and, of Thy great goodness, keep us alive through this dying life, that out of death Thou mayest raise us up to immortality. For His sake who is the Life, Jesus Christ our Lord—Amen.

Christina G. Rossetti.

O God, who hast taught us to keep all Thy heavenly commandments by loving Thee and our neighbor; grant us the spirit of peace and grace, that we may be both devoted to Thee with our whole heart, and united to each other with a pure will; through Jesus Christ our Lord—Amen.

Leonine Sacramentary, A. D. 460.

Lord! when I am in sorrow I think on Thee. Listen to the cry of my heart, and my sorrowful complaint. Yet, O Father, I would not prescribe to Thee when and how Thy help should come. I will willingly tarry for the hour which Thou Thyself hast appointed for my relief. Meanwhile strengthen me by Thy Holy Spirit; strengthen my faith, my hope, my trust; give me patience and resolution to bear my trouble; and let me at last behold the time when Thou wilt make me glad with Thy grace. Ah, my Father! never yet hast Thou forsaken Thy children, forsake not me. Ever dost Thou give gladness unto the sorrowful, O give it now unto me. Always dost Thou relieve the wretched, relieve me too, when and where and how Thou wilt. Unto Thy wisdom, love, and goodness, I leave it utterly— Amen.

J. F. Stark (1680–1756).

Eternal God, Fountain of all love, trusting in Thy love, I come before Thee, to speak to Thee, to ask Thee for Thy love. Thou knowest all I would ask Thee if I dared; Thou knowest how I would love Thee if I could; Thou knowest all I would hope of Thee, if mine own unworthiness did not keep me back. Yet Thou givest me the longing, Thou wilt give what I long for, even Thyself, whom I long for. Thou preparest the heart. Prepare my heart, O loving God, that I may long for Thee more, adore Thee more humbly, ask at least, with all the desires of my heart, all which Thou art ready to give me, which Thou hast prepared for me, if I love Thee. Make me to love Thee through all Thy love for me, through Thine own love in me—Amen.

E. B. Pusey.

My Lord, abide with me, I beseech Thee, and in Thee let my soul find rest, and let it delight itself in Thee, for what is there that can be compared with that peace which is in Thee, seeing that it passeth all understanding! Nothing can bring me any good if I lack Thy peace. And what can I lack if I have Thee, who art all Good? I will rejoice in Thee, and Thou, I hope and pray most humbly, wilt disperse this cloud, and wilt show me the light of Thy will, and wilt cause Thy peace and serenity to fill and gladden my heart. Verily, the heart is ever restless, until it rest in Thee alone. It, which can contain the Highest Good, can never be filled or satisfied with aught that is less than Thee—Amen.

The Way of Eternal Life.

November the Fourteenth + + + 319

O **Lord of life, and Lord of love!** love us into life, and give us life to love Thee. Grant us life enough to put life into all things, that when we travel o'er this part of our life, and it seems but dust and barrenness, we may be of those who hope in Thee. Touch this barrenness, till all things bloom. Touch those of us whose life is barrenner than it need be—lacking knowledge and beauty, filled with petty interests and foolish cares. Lord, forgive us that our life is so poor, and grant us the thoughts of God, that we may be enabled for the time to come to make this very desert blossom as the rose. Grant that in us, short-lived, vexed with cares, hungry, thirsty, dying, the Spirit of God may so come and so dwell, that the beauty of the Lord may be upon us, and the work of our hands be established : through Jesus Christ our Lord—Amen.

George Dawson.

I Beseech Thee, my most gracious God, preserve me from the cares of this life, lest I should be too much entangled therein; also from the many necessities of the body, lest I should be ensnared by pleasure; and from whatsoever is an obstacle to the soul, lest, being broken with troubles, I should be overthrown. Give me strength to resist, patience to endure, and constancy to persevere—Amen.

Thomas à Kempis.

O God, who purifiest the heart of man from sin, and makest it more white than snow, pour down upon us the abundance of Thy mercy; renew, we beseech Thee, Thy Holy Spirit within us, that we may show forth Thy praise, and strengthened by Thy grace, may obtain rest in the eternal mansions of the heavenly Jerusalem: through our Lord Jesus Christ—Amen.

Sarum Breviary, A.D. 1085.

November the Sixteenth ✛ ✢ ✢ ✢ 321

Merciful Lord God, O Lord most merciful, so replenish us with grace that, whatever else may be hidden from us, we may always, everywhere, and in all things, discern Thy mercy. For if being Truth Thou canst not deny Thyself, neither being Love canst Thou be other than Thyself. In which Thine unchangeableness, grant us quiet hearts, assurance of holy hope, peace, patient confidence of love. For Jesus Christ's sake—Amen.

Christina G. Rossetti.

Lord, who hast taught us that all our doings without charity are nothing worth, send Thy Holy Spirit and pour into our hearts that most excellent gift of charity, the very bond of peace and of all virtues, without which whosoever liveth is counted dead before Thee. Grant this for Thine only Son Jesus Christ's sake—Amen.

Book of Common Prayer, A. D. 1549.

322 ✢ ✢ ✢ November the Seventeenth

h, give me light to see, a heart to close with, and power to do Thy will, O God—Amen.

Thomas Wilson (1663-1775).

Almighty God, and most merciful Father, give us, we beseech Thee, that grace that we may duly examine the inmost of our hearts, and our most secret thoughts, how we stand before Thee; and that we may henceforward never be drawn to do any thing that may dishonor Thy name: but may persevere in all good purposes, and in Thy holy service, unto our lives' end; and grant that we may now this present day, seeing it is as good as nothing that we have done hitherto, perfectly begin to walk before Thee, as becometh those that are called to an inheritance of light in Christ—Amen.

Hickes' Devotions, 1700.

November the Eighteenth ✦ ✦ ✦ ✦ 323

O God, animate us to cheerfulness. May we have a joyful sense of our blessings, learn to look on the bright circumstances of our lot, and maintain a perpetual contentedness under Thy allotments. Fortify our minds against disappointment and calamity. Preserve us from despondency, from yielding to dejection. Teach us that no evil is intolerable but a guilty conscience; and that nothing can hurt us, if, with true loyalty of affection, we keep Thy commandments, and take refuge in Thee—Amen.

William Ellery Channing.

We give Thee thanks, Holy Lord, Father Almighty, everlasting God, who hast been pleased to bring us through the night to the hours of morning; we pray Thee to grant us to pass this day without sin, so that at eventide we may again give thanks to Thee; through Jesus Christ our Lord—Amen. Gelasian, A. D. 492.

November the Nineteenth

O Lord God Almighty, who givest power to the faint, and increasest strength to them that have no might! Without Thee I can do nothing, but by Thy gracious assistance I am enabled for the performance of every duty laid upon me. Lord of power and love! I come, trusting in Thine almighty strength, and Thine infinite goodness, to beg from Thee what is wanting in myself; even that grace which shall help me such to be, and such to do, as Thou wouldest have me. O my God! let Thy grace be sufficient for me, and ever present with me, that I may do all things as I ought. I will trust in Thee, in whom is everlasting strength. Be Thou my Helper, to carry me on beyond my own strength, and to make all that I think, and speak, and do, acceptable in Thy sight, through Jesus Christ —Amen.

Benjamin Jenks (1646-1724)

November the Twentieth

 O God, who art the Fountain of Truth and the Giver of spiritual knowledge, who leadest us from year to year in unchanging love —we bless Thee that, when by sight we could not gaze upon Thy glory, by faith we can know Thee, and lay hold on that Truth which giveth light to the soul. Especially do we thank Thee for Him in whom the true light shineth on every man that cometh into the world. And we ask from the treasures of Thy grace for a more childlike trust, a more faithful spirit, a more loyal will. May our obedience open to us all spiritual knowledge. May the truth of our own lives lead us into communion with Thy spirit of Truth. May we be transformed into the likeness of Christ, and so renew Thine image on the earth, and hasten the coming of that kingdom of truth and liberty and love— Amen.

Henry W. Foote.

O Lord, may Thy all-powerful grace make me as perfect as Thou hast commanded me to be—Amen.

Thomas Wilson (1663-1755).

O Most merciful God, whose mercies are as high as the heavens, great and many as the moments of eternity; fill my soul, I beseech Thee, with great thoughts of Thy unspeakable blessings, that my thankfulness may be as great as my needs of mercy are. Let Thy loving-kindness endure for ever and ever upon me; and, because I cannot praise Thee according to Thy excellence, take my soul, in due time, into the land of everlasting praises, that I may spend a whole eternity in ascribing to Thy Name praise, and honor, and dominion. Grant this for Jesus Christ's sake—Amen.

Jeremy Taylor (1613-1667).

November the Twenty-second ✤ ✤ 327

Grant us peace, and establish Thy truth in us; as Thou fillest all things living with plenteousness.

Remember every faithful soul in trial; and comfort, if it be possible, every one in sorrow and distress.

O Helper of the helpless, bring the wanderer home, and give health to the sick, and deliverance to the captive.

Sustain the aged, comfort the weakhearted, set free those whose souls are bound in misery and iron; remember all those that are in affliction, necessity, and emergency everywhere.

Let us dwell with Thee in peace, as children of light; and in Thy light, Lord, let us see the light.

Direct, O Lord, in peace, the close of our life; trustfully, fearlessly, and, if it be Thy will, painlessly. Gather us when Thou wilt, into the abodes of Thy chosen; without shame, or stain, or sin—Amen.

Rowland Williams.

328 ✦ ✦ November the Twenty-third

Look upon us and hear us, O Lord our God; and assist those endeavors to please Thee which Thou Thyself hast granted to us; as Thou hast given the first act of will, so give the completion of the work; grant that we may be able to finish what Thou hast granted us to wish to begin—Amen.

Mozarabic, before A. D. 700.

O God, who hast taught us to do unto others as we would they should do unto us; give me grace to cleanse my heart and hands from all fraud and wrong, that I may hurt nobody by word or deed, but be true and just in all my dealings; that so, keeping innocency and taking heed unto the thing that is right, I may have peace at the last; through Jesus Christ our Lord—Amen.

Pocket Manual of Prayers, 1860.

November the Twenty-fourth ✢ ✢ 329

 **Lord, Creator of all things,** be gracious, I entreat Thee, unto all Thy creatures. Give us all grace to serve Thee in our appointed place, rejoicing before Thee to Thy praise; each fulfilling the law under which Thou bringest him, each glorifying Thee according to the special excellence Thou bestowest—Amen.

Christina G. Rossetti.

Most great and glorious God, who hast appointed the rivers to hasten with a rapid motion to the sea, be graciously pleased, I most humbly beseech Thee, to make the stream of my will perpetually to flow a cheerful and impetuous course, bearing down pleasure, interest, afflictions, death, and all other obstacles and impediments whatsoever, before it, till it plunge itself joyfully into the unfathomable ocean of Thy divine will, for the sake of Thy beloved Son, my Saviour, Jesus Christ—Amen.

Charles How (1661-1745).

Bless and sanctify my soul with Thy heavenly blessings, that it may become Thy holy habitation, and let nothing be found in this temple of Thy Divinity, which shall offend the eyes of Thy Majesty. According to the greatness of Thy goodness and multitude of Thy mercies, look upon me, and hear the prayer of Thy poor servant. Protect and keep my soul, amidst so many dangers of this life, and, by Thy grace accompanying me, direct it along the way of peace, to its home of everlasting brightness—Amen.

Thomas à Kempis.

O God, who tellest the number of the stars, and callest them all by their names; heal, we beseech Thee, the contrite in heart, and gather together the outcasts, and enrich us with the fulness of Thy wisdom; through Christ our Lord—Amen.

Sarum Breviary, A.D. 1085.

November the Twenty-sixth ✦ ✦ 331

 Thou who art Love, and who seest all the suffering, injustice and misery which reign in this world, have pity, we implore Thee, on the work of Thy hands. Look mercifully upon the poor, the oppressed, and all who are heavy laden with error, labor, and sorrow. Fill our hearts with deep compassion for those who suffer, and hasten the coming of Thy kingdom of justice and truth—Amen.

Eugène Bersier.

Almighty and everlasting God, the Comfort of the sad, the Strength of sufferers, let the prayers of those that cry out of any tribulation come unto Thee; that all may rejoice to find that Thy mercy is present with them in their afflictions; through Jesus Christ our Lord—Amen.

Gelasian, A. D. 492.

Open Thou my heart for Thy love, keep Thy love in me, prepare me by Thy love for greater fulness of Thy love, until I have reached the fullest measure of love, which Thou, in Thine eternal love, hast willed for me.

Make me, in thought, word, and deed, to love Thee, and thank Thee, and praise Thee, and praising Thee to love Thee more, and know Thee more, how worthy Thou art of all love and praise, until I be fitted with all Thy saints and angels to love Thee and praise Thee everlastingly, and breathe out my soul to Thee in loving Thee and praising Thee for all Thy boundless, undeserved love to me, Thy poor sinner, yet, though a sinner, Thine, O God my God—Amen.

E. B. Pusey.

November the Twenty-eighth ✦ ✦ 333

O Lord our God, keep us from all darkness except such as our own foolishness brings over us. Let us remember that there is no darkness with Thee. Let us have but one thing to be afraid of—the death of the spirit. Let there be but one thing that we shrink from—unlovingness towards Thee and our brother. And when the storm is loud, and the night is dark, and the soul is sad, and the heart oppressed ; then, as weary travelers, may we look to Thee; and beholding the light of Thy love, may it bear us on, until we learn to sing Thy song in the night. And when the last chill stream of death shall be crossed, grant that ours may be the Delectable Mountains, the company of faithful souls, the eternal years, the everlasting life. Of Thy great mercy hear our supplications, through Jesus Christ our Lord—Amen.

George Dawson.

November the Twenty-ninth

I know, O Lord, Thou wilt do Thy part towards me, as I, through Thy grace, desire to do my part towards Thee. I know well Thou canst never forsake those who seek Thee, nor disappoint those who trust Thee. Yet I know too, the more I pray for Thy protection, the more surely and fully I shall have it. And therefore now I cry out to Thee, and entreat Thee, first that Thou wouldest keep me from myself, and from following any will but Thine. Next, I beg of Thee that, in Thine infinite compassion, Thou wouldest temper Thy will to me. Visit me not, O my loving Lord—if it be not wrong so to pray,—visit me not with those trying visitations which saints alone can bear! Pity my weakness, and lead me heavenwards in a safe and tranquil course. Still I leave all in Thy hands,—only, if Thou shalt bring heavier trials on me, give me more grace, flood me with the fulness of Thy strength and consolation—Amen.

John Henry Newman.

November the Thirtieth ✚ ✚ ✚ ✚ 335

God, the Father of the forsaken, the Help of the weak, the Supplier of the needy, who hast diffused and proportioned Thy gifts to body and soul, in such sort that all may acknowledge and perform the joyous duty of mutual service; who teachest us that love towards the race of man is the bond of perfectness, and the imitation of Thy blessed self; open our eyes and touch our hearts, that we may see and do, both for this world and for that which is to come, the things which belong unto our peace. Strengthen me in the work I have undertaken; give me counsel and wisdom, perseverance, faith and zeal, and in Thine own good time, and according to Thy pleasure, prosper the issue. Pour into me a spirit of humility; let nothing be done but in devout obedience to Thy will, thankfulness for Thine unspeakable mercies, and love to Thine adorable Son Christ Jesus—Amen.

Antony Ashley Cooper, Earl of Shaftesbury
(1801–1885).

Thou, O Lord, who commandest me to ask, grant that I may receive; Thou hast put me upon seeking, let me be happy in finding; Thou hast bidden me knock, I pray Thee open unto me. Be graciously pleased to direct and govern all my thoughts and actions, that, for the future, I may serve Thee, and entirely devote myself to obeying Thee. Accept me, I beseech Thee, and draw me to Thyself, that I may henceforth be Thine by obedience and love, who am already all Thine own, as Thy creature. Even Thine, O Lord, who livest and reignest for ever and ever—Amen.

St. Augustine (354-430).

Lord, take my lips, and speak through them; take my mind, and think through it; take my heart, and set it on fire—Amen.

W. H. H. Aitken.

December the Second ✦ ✦ ✦ ✦ ✦ 337

Lord, be with my spirit, and dwell in my heart by faith. Oh, make me such as I should be towards Thee, and such as Thou mayest take pleasure in me. Be with me everywhere and at all times, in all events and circumstances of my life; to sanctify and sweeten to me whatever befalls me; and never leave nor forsake me in my present pilgrimage here, till Thou hast brought me safe through all trials and dangers to be ever with Thee, there to live in Thy sight and love, world without end—Amen.

Benjamin Jenks (1646-1724).

O Thou that enlightenest every man that cometh into the world, enlighten our hearts with the brightness of Thy grace, that we may ponder and love those things that are acceptable unto Thee—Amen.

Priest's Prayer Book.

December the Third

Be Thou favorable unto me, merciful, sweet, and gracious Lord, and grant to me, Thy poor needy creature, sometimes at least to feel, if it be but a small portion, of Thy hearty affectionate love; that my faith may become more strong, my hope in Thy goodness may be increased, and that love, once kindled within me, may never fail—Amen.

Thomas à Kempis.

Give me, Lord, I pray Thee, the grace and virtue of constancy, and unwearied endurance, that so I may receive with thanksgiving whatever Thy hand may send of calamity or distress in this life, may bear it patiently, overcome it manfully, and, in every change and chance of life may, with simple trust and resignation, cast myself and all I have into the arms of Thy good Providence—Amen.

Paradise for the Christian Soul.

December the Fourth ✠ ✠ ✠ ✠ ✠ 339

Grant unto us, O Lord, the spirit of mutual love and duty, and, above all, of grateful obedience to Thee; give us comfort and support under all circumstances of our life, and Thy merciful guidance unto the end; that, living in all holy and godly conversation, we may be afflicted by no adversity, and may finally attain to the perpetual enjoyment of Thy loving mercy; through Jesus Christ our Lord—Amen.

James Skinner (1818-1882).

Thou, our Lord and our God, our merciful Father in Heaven, we entreat Thee with childlike hearts, give us in this world whatever is really good and happy for us in soul and body, according to Thy holy will and pleasure. May we live as Christians, endure with patience, and at last die in peace and hope, for Jesus Christ's sake—Amen.

Johann Quirsfeld (1641-1686).

340 ✢ ✢ ✢ ✢ ✢ ✢ December the Fifth

Speak, Lord, for Thy servant heareth. Grant us ears to hear, eyes to see, wills to obey, hearts to love; then declare what Thou wilt, reveal what Thou wilt, command what Thou wilt, demand what Thou wilt—Amen.

Christina G. Rossetti.

Eternal God, make my body and soul to be a holy temple, purified for the habitation of Thy Holy Spirit. Cast out of it, O Lord, all worldly affections, all covetous desires; let it be a place of prayer and holy meditation; of pure intentions, and zealous desires of pleasing Thee; so that, loving Thee above all the world, and worshipping Thee continually in humblest adoration, I may be prepared to glorify Thee to all eternity in heaven; through Jesus Christ our Lord—Amen.

Jeremy Taylor (1613–1667).

December the Sixth   341

Grant unto us, Almighty God, Thy peace that passeth understanding; that we, amid the storms and troubles of this our life, may rest in Thee, knowing that all things are in Thee, under Thy care, governed by Thy will, guarded by Thy love; so that with a quiet heart we may see the storms of life, the cloud and the thick darkness; ever rejoicing to know that the darkness and the light are both alike to Thee. Guide, guard, and govern us even to the end, that none of us may fail to lay hold upon the immortal life—Amen.

George Dawson.

Lighten our darkness, we beseech Thee, O Lord; and by Thy great mercy defend us from all perils and dangers of this night; for the love of Thy only Son, our Saviour, Jesus Christ—Amen.

Gelasian, A. D. 492.

Behold, O Father of mercies, I resign myself and all that I have unto Thee. I rely upon Thy bounty for what Thou judgest fit and needful for me. Thy truth and faithfulness is my best security; Thy wisdom is my satisfaction in all events and accidents; Thy power is my support, protection, and safeguard. Lead me whither Thou pleasest; and I will follow Thee with a cheerful heart. I refuse nothing which comes from Thy hands, O most loving Father. I submit to Thy orders, and hope that all things shall work together for my good. And I trust in Thy grace, that I shall always do as I do now, steadfastly adhering thus unto Thee, and never suffering anything that befalls me to pull me away from this humble faith in Thy wise and almighty goodness—Amen.

Simon Patrick (1626–1707).

December the Eighth ✦ ✦ ✦ ✦ ✦ 343

My God, Thou and Thou alone art all-wise and all-knowing! I believe that Thou knowest just what is best for me. I believe that Thou lovest me better than I love myself, that Thou art all-wise in Thy Providence and all-powerful in Thy protection. I thank Thee, with all my heart, that Thou hast taken me out of my own keeping, and hast bidden me to put myself in Thy hands. I can ask nothing better than this, to be Thy care, not my own. O my Lord, through Thy grace, I will follow Thee whithersoever Thou goest, and will not lead the way. I will wait on Thee for Thy guidance, and, on obtaining it, I will act in simplicity and without fear. And I promise that I will not be impatient, if at any time I am kept by Thee in darkness and perplexity; nor will I complain or fret if I come into any misfortune or anxiety— Amen.

John Henry Newman.

**O God, the Father of Lights,** from whom cometh down every good and perfect gift; mercifully look upon our frailty and infirmity, and grant us such health of body as Thou knowest to be needful for us; that, both in our bodies and souls, we may evermore serve Thee with all our strength and might; through Jesus Christ our Lord—Amen.

Private Devotions, 1560.

O God our Father, who dost exhort us to pray, and who dost grant what we ask, if only, when we ask, we live a better life; hear me, who am trembling in this darkness, and stretch forth Thy hand unto me; hold forth Thy light before me; recall me from my wanderings; and, Thou being my Guide, may I be restored to myself and to Thee, through Jesus Christ —Amen.

St. Augustine (354-430).

December the Tenth 345

 **Holy and loving Father, whose** mercies are from everlasting to everlasting, we thank Thee that Thy children can flee for refuge in their afflictions to the blessed certainty of Thy love. From every grief that burdens our spirits, from the sense of solitude and loss, from the doubt and fainting of the soul in its trouble, we turn to Thee. Thou knowest our frame, Thou rememberest that we are dust. Be Thou our Strength and Deliverer; in our great need be Thou our Helper; pour Thy consolations into our hearts, and let the gospel of Thy beloved Son minister comfort and peace to our souls—Amen.

Henry W. Foote.

 **God Almighty, who to them** that have no might increasest strength, strengthen us to do and suffer Thy good will and pleasure; through Jesus Christ—Amen.

Christina G. Rossetti.

O God, the Creator of both summer and winter, who causest light to shine out of the thick gloom, and bringest good out of evil; give us grace so to flee what Thou forbiddest, that we may cast aside the works of darkness, and so to choose what Thou commandest, that we may be children of light; but, since darkness and light obey Thee, give all the messengers of Thy Providence charge over us, that, serving Thee in peace and thankfulness, we may be brought through humility to serve Thee in glory—Amen.

Rowland Williams.

Most gracious God, to know and love whose will is righteousness, enlighten our souls with the brightness of Thy presence, that we may both know Thy will, and be enabled to perform it—Amen.

Roman Breviary.

December the Twelfth ✦ ✦ ✦ ✦ ✦ 347

Omost loving Lord, I offer my whole self unto Thee. Take, I pray Thee, into the hands of Thine unspeakable pity, both my soul and body, my senses, words, and actions; vouchsafe in all things so to direct and govern me, that I may ever flee every occasion of sin, and may so constantly cleave to Thee and to Thy commandments, that neither life nor death, nor anything which may befall me, may separate me from Thee—Amen.

Treasury of Devotion, 1869.

Almighty God, who hast planted the Day-star in the heavens, and, scattering the night, dost restore morning to the world; fill us, we beseech Thee, with Thy mercy, so that, Thou being our Enlightener, all the darkness of our sins may be dispersed, through our Lord Jesus Christ —Amen.

Sarum Breviary, A. D. 1085.

 Almighty God, Father and Lord of all the creatures, who hast disposed all things and all chances so as may best magnify Thy mercy, bringing good out of evil; I most humbly beseech Thee to give me wisdom from above, that I may adore Thee and admire Thy ways and footsteps, which are in the great deep and not to be searched out; teach me to submit to Thy Providence in all things, to be content in all changes of person and condition, to be temperate in prosperity, and to read my duty in the lines of Thy mercy; and in adversity to be meek, patient, and resigned; and to look through the cloud, that I may wait for the consolation of the Lord; in the meantime doing my duty with an unwearied diligence, and an undisturbed resolution, being strengthened with the spirit of the inner man; through Jesus Christ our Lord—Amen.

Jeremy Taylor (1613-1667).

December the Fourteenth 349

O Thou divine Spirit, let me find my strength in Thee. I need Thee, that I may be strong everywhere. I long to be independent of all circumstances, alike of the cloud and of the sunshine. I want a power to save me from sinking in despondency, and to rescue me from soaring in pride. I want both a pillar of fire and a pillar of cloud; a refuge from the night of adversity, and a shield from the day of prosperity. I can find them in Thee. Thou hast proved Thy power both over the night and over the day. Come into my heart, and Thy power shall be my power. I shall be victorious over all circumstances, at home in all scenes, restful in all fortunes. I shall have power to tread upon scorpions, and they shall do me no hurt; the world shall be mine when Thy Spirit is in me— Amen.

George Matheson.

O Lord my God, be not Thou far from me; my God, have regard to help me; for there have risen up against me sundry thoughts, and great fears, afflicting my soul. How shall I pass through unhurt? how shall I break them to pieces? This is my hope, my one only consolation, to flee unto Thee in every tribulation, to trust in Thee, to call upon Thee from my inmost heart, and to wait patiently for Thy consolation—Amen.

Thomas à Kempis.

Almighty and most merciful God, of Thy bountiful goodness keep us, we beseech Thee, from all things that may hurt us; that we, being ready both in body and soul, may cheerfully accomplish those things which Thou commandest; through Jesus Christ our Lord—Amen.

Gelasian, A. D. 492.

December the Sixteenth

Almighty Lord our God, direct our steps into the way of peace, and strengthen our hearts to obey Thy commands; may the Day-spring visit us from on high, and give light to those who sit in darkness and the shadow of death; that they may adore Thee for Thy mercy, follow Thee for Thy truth, desire Thee for Thy sweetness, who art the blessed Lord God of Israel—Amen.

Ancient Collect.

O God of patience and consolation, give us such good-will, we beseech Thee, that with free hearts we may love and serve Thee and our brethren; and, having thus the mind of Christ, may begin heaven on earth, and exercise ourselves therein till that day when heaven where love abideth shall seem no strange habitation to us. For Jesus Christ's sake—Amen.

Christina G. Rossetti.

Almighty and merciful God, who art the Strength of the weak, the Refreshment of the weary, the Comfort of the sad, the Help of the tempted, the Life of the dying, the God of patience and of all consolation; Thou knowest full well the inner weakness of our nature, how we tremble and quiver before pain, and cannot bear the cross without Thy Divine help and support. Help me, then, O eternal and pitying God, help me to possess my soul in patience, to maintain unshaken hope in Thee, to keep that childlike trust which feels a Father's heart hidden beneath the cross; so shall I be strengthened with power according to Thy glorious might, in all patience and long-suffering; I shall be enabled to endure pain and temptation, and, in the very depth of my suffering, to praise Thee with a joyful heart.
—Amen.

Johann Habermann (1516–1590).

December the Eighteenth ✦ ✦ ✦ ✦ 353

Eternal Light, before whom all darkness is light, and, in comparison with whom, every other light is but darkness! May it please Thee to send forth Thy light and Thy truth, that they may lead us. Purify, we pray Thee, our souls from all impure imaginations, that Thy most beautiful and holy image may be again renewed within us, and, by contemplating Thy glorious perfections, we may feel daily improved within us that Divine similitude, the perfection whereof we hope will at last make us forever happy in that full and beatific vision we aspire after. Till this most blessed day break, and the shadows fly away, let Thy Spirit be continually with us, and may we feel the powerful effects of Thy Divine grace constantly directing and supporting our steps; that all our endeavors, throughout the whole remaining part of our lives, may serve to promote the honor of Thy blessed Name, through Jesus Christ our Lord—Amen.

Robert Leighton (1611–1684).

December the Nineteenth

**Blessed Lord, who hast commanded** us to love one another, grant us grace that, having received Thine undeserved bounty, we may love every one in Thee and for Thee. We implore Thy clemency for all; but especially for the friends whom Thy love has given to us. Love Thou them, O Thou Fountain of love, and make them to love Thee with all their heart, that they may will, and speak, and do those things only which are pleasing to Thee—Amen.

St. Anselm (1033–1109).

Grant us, O Lord, to pass this day in gladness and peace, without stumbling and without stain; that, reaching the eventide victorious over all temptation, we may praise Thee, the eternal God, who art blessed, and dost govern all things, world without end—Amen.

Mozarabic, before A. D. 700.

December the Twentieth ✦ ✦ ✦ ✦ 355

O **My God, bestow upon us such** confidence, such peace, such happiness in Thee, that Thy will may always be dearer to us than our own will, and Thy pleasure than our own pleasure. All that Thou givest is Thy free gift to us, all that Thou takest away Thy grace to us. Be Thou thanked for all, praised for all, loved for all; through Jesus Christ our Lord—Amen.

Christina G. Rossetti.

A **Almighty God, who alone canst** order the unruly wills and affections of sinful men, grant unto Thy people, that they may love the thing which Thou commandest, and desire that which Thou dost promise; that so, among the sundry and manifold changes of the world, our hearts may surely there be fixed, where true joys are to be found; through Jesus Christ our Lord—Amen.

Gelasian Sacramentary, A. D. 492.
Altered in 1662.

December the Twenty-first

Write **Thy blessed name, O Lord,** upon my heart, there to remain so indelibly engraven, that no prosperity, no adversity shall ever move me from Thy love. Be Thou to me a strong Tower of defence, a Comforter in tribulation, a Deliverer in distress, a very present Help in trouble, and a Guide to heaven through the many temptations and dangers of this life— Amen.

Thomas à Kempis.

Enlarge **our souls with a divine** charity, that we may hope all things, endure all things; and become messengers of Thy healing mercy to the grievances and infirmities of men. In all things attune our hearts to the holiness and harmony of Thy kingdom. And hasten the time when Thy kingdom shall come, and Thy will be done on earth as it is in heaven— Amen.

James Martineau.

December the Twenty-second ✤ ✤ 357

As Thou makest the outgoings of the morning and evening to rejoice, so lift up the light of Thy countenance upon us, and make us glad with the tokens of Thy love. Be Thou with us, O Lord, and let Thy grace follow us this day, and all the days of our life. Be Thou our Guide unto death, in death our Comfort, and, after death, our Portion and Happiness everlasting— Amen.

Benjamin Jenks.

O God, who art the Author of peace and Lover of concord, in knowledge of whom standeth our eternal life, whose service is perfect freedom; defend us Thy humble servants in all assaults of our enemies, that we, surely trusting in Thy defence, may not fear the power of any adversaries, through the might of Jesus Christ our Lord—Amen.

Gelasian Sacramentary, A. D. 494.

December the Twenty-third

Almighty God, Giver of all good, who hast given, above all Thy gifts, the crowning mercy that we are called in Christ Jesus to know and love and serve Thee, we would bring Thee thanks and praises for the Divine Light which reveals the heart of grace in Thy leading of souls and peoples. Help us to rise to a fit gratitude for the overrunning blessings which Thou givest ever, even to the darkest lot and life,—the temporal felicities, the Divine comforts, the eternal hopes. That all things are of Thy mercy, by Thy mercy, and in Thy mercy, we thank Thee. Make us to sing Thy song in the light, and in the night to touch Thy hand and be at peace. Grant, we pray, with all other blessings, Thy best gifts, thankful and trustful hearts, that Thou mayest be our Lord and King for evermore— Amen.

Henry W. Foote.

December the Twenty-fourth + + 359

Our Heavenly Father we rejoice in the blessed communion of all Thy saints, wherein Thou givest us also to have part. We remember before Thee all who have departed this life in Thy faith and love, and especially those most dear to us. We thank Thee for our present fellowship with them, for our common hope, and for the promise of future joy. Oh, let the cloud of witnesses, the innumerable company of those who have gone before, and entered into rest, be to us for an example of godly life, and even now may we be refreshed with their joy; that so with patience we may run the race that yet remains before us, looking unto Jesus the author and finisher of our faith; and obtain an entrance into the everlasting kingdom, the glorious assembly of the saints, and with them ever worship and adore Thy glorious Name, world without end—Amen.

Book of Prayers, 1851.

Almighty God, we give Thee thanks for the mighty yearning of the human heart for the coming of a Saviour, and the constant promise of Thy Word that He was to come. In our own souls we repeat the humble sighs and panting aspirations of ancient men and ages, and own that our souls are in darkness and infirmity without faith in Him who comes to bring God to man and man to God. We bless Thee for the tribute that we can pay to Him from our very sense of need and dependence, and that our own hearts can so answer from their wilderness, the cry, "Prepare ye the way of the Lord." In us the rough places are to be made smooth, the crooked straight, the mountains of pride brought low, and the valleys of despondency lifted up. O God, prepare Thou the way in us now, and may we welcome anew Thy Holy Child. Hosanna! blessed be he who cometh in the name of the Lord—Amen.

Samuel Osgood, 1862.

December the Twenty-sixth ✢ ✢ ✢ 361

O Lord, who hast breathed into me the breath of life, and endued me with an immortal spirit, which looks up unto Thee, and remembers it is made after Thine own image, behold with grace and favor the ardent desires which are in mine heart, to recover a perfect likeness of Thee. Endue me with more contentedness in what is present, and less solicitude about what is future; with a patient mind to submit to any loss of what I have, or to any disappointment of what I expect. Fill me, O Lord, with the knowledge of Thy will, in all wisdom and spiritual understanding. Fill me with goodness, and the fruits of righteousness. And fill me with all joy and peace in believing that Thou wilt never leave me nor forsake me, but make me perfect, stablish, strengthen, settle me, and be my God for ever and ever; my Guide even unto death—Amen.

Simon Patrick (1626–1707).

Gracious Lord, in whom are laid up all the treasures of knowledge and wisdom, direct me in the ways of life; remove from me the ways of death. Give me a soft and meek spirit, that I may help the succorless, and comfort the comfortless. O my dear Lord, pardon me for the neglect of this duty, and make me to redeem the time with a cheerful constancy—Amen.

The Penitent Pilgrim, 1641.

We entreat Thy mercy with our whole heart, that, as Thou defendest us against things adverse to the body, so Thou wilt set us free from the enemies of the soul; and, as Thou grantest us to rejoice in outward tranquillity, so vouchsafe to us Thine inward peace; through Jesus Christ our Lord—Amen.

Leonine Sacramentary, A. D. 440.

December the Twenty-eighth ✠ ✠ 363

God, who hast enkindled in the holy bosoms of all Thy saints so great an ardor of faith, that they despised all bodily pains, while hastening with all earnestness to Thee, the Author of life; hear our prayers, and grant that the hateful sweetness of sin may wax faint in us, and we may glow with the infused warmth of love for Thee; through Thy mercy, O our God, who art blessed, and dost live, and govern all things, world without end—Amen.

Mozarabic, before A. D. 700.

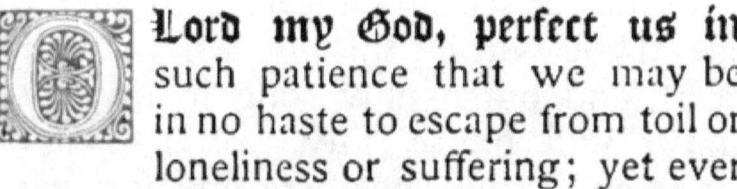Lord my God, perfect us in such patience that we may be in no haste to escape from toil or loneliness or suffering; yet ever in haste to serve Thee, to please Thee, and, when Thou wilt, to go home to Thy blessed Presence—Amen.

Christina G. Rossetti.

364 ✠ ✠ December the Twenty-ninth

Ah, God! behold my grief and care. Fain would I serve Thee with a glad and cheerful countenance, but I cannot do it. However much I fight and struggle against my sadness, I am too weak for this sore conflict. Help me in my weakness, O Thou mighty God! and give me Thy Holy Spirit to refresh and comfort me in my sorrow. Amid all my fears and griefs I yet know that I am Thine in life and death, and that nothing can really part me from Thee; neither things present, nor things to come, neither trial, nor fear, nor pain. And therefore, O Lord, I will still trust in Thy grace. Thou wilt not send me away unheard. Sooner or later Thou wilt lift this burden from my heart, and put a new song in my lips; and I will praise Thy goodness, and thank and serve Thee here and for evermore—Amen.

S. Scherertz (1584-1639).

December the Thirtieth

Heavenly and eternal Father, Source of all being, from whom I spring, unto whom I shall re-return,—Thine I shall ever be. Thou wilt call me unto Thyself when my hour comes. Blessed shall I then be if I can say, "I have fought a good fight." I fear not death, O Father of life; for death is not eternal sleep; it is the transition to a new life, a moment of glorious transformation, an ascension towards Thee. How could that be an evil that cometh from Thy hand, when Thou art the All-good! Lord of life and death, I am in Thy hand; do unto me as Thou deemest fit; for what Thou dost is well done. When Thou didst call me from nothing into life, Thou didst will my happiness; when Thou callest me away from life, will my happiness be less Thy care? No, no, Thou art love, and whosoever dwells in love, dwells in Thee, O Lord, and Thou in him—Amen.

Heinrich Tschokke (1771–1848).

Most gracious God, who hast been infinitely merciful to us, not only in the year past, but through all the years of our life, be pleased to accept our most unfeigned thanks for Thine innumerable blessings to us; graciously pardoning the manifold sins and infirmities of our life past, and bountifully bestowing upon us all those graces and virtues, which may render us acceptable to Thee. And, every year which Thou shalt be pleased to add to our lives, add also, we humbly implore Thee, more strength to our faith, more ardor to our love, and a greater perfection to our obedience; and grant that, in a humble sincerity and constant perseverance, we may serve Thee most faithfully the remainder of our lives, for Jesus Christ's sake—Amen.

Charles How (1661–1745).

www.ingramcontent.com/pod-product-compliance
Lightning Source LLC
Chambersburg PA
CBHW030344230426
43664CB00007BB/533